Rick Steves'

SNAPSHOT

Italy's Cinque Terre

CONTENTS

INTRODUCTION

This Snapshot guide, excerpted from the latest edition of my guidebook *Rick Steves' Italy,* introduces you to my favorite stretch of the Italian Riviera. The Cinque Terre—literally "five lands"—is a charm bracelet of picturesque, traffic-free villages where you can melt into small-town Italy. Sit on the breakwater to enjoy the views, hike the scenic trails between the villages, and dine on a succulent seafood feast as you hear the roar of the surf. I've also included coverage of nearby Riviera destinations, including the beach towns of Levanto, Sestri Levante, the larger Santa Margherita Ligure, trendier Portofino, resorty Portovenere, and the workaday transportation hub of La Spezia.

To help you have the best trip possible, I've included the following topics in this book:

• **Planning Your Time,** with advice on how to make the most of your limited time

• **Orientation,** including tourist information (abbreviated as TI), tips on public transportation, local tour options, and helpful hints

• **Sights** with ratings:

▲▲▲—Don't miss

▲▲—Try hard to see

▲—Worthwhile if you can make it

No rating—Worth knowing about

• **Sleeping** and **Eating,** with good-value recommendations in every price range

• **Connections,** with tips on trains, buses, and driving

• **Practicalities,** near the end of this book, has information on money, phoning, hotel reservations, transportation, and other helpful hints, plus Italian survival phrases.

To travel smartly, read this little book in its entirety before you go. It's my hope that this guide will make your trip more meaningful and rewarding. Traveling like a temporary local, you'll get the absolute most out of every mile, minute, and euro.

Buon viaggio!

Rick Steves

THE CINQUE TERRE

The Cinque Terre (CHINK-weh TAY-reh), a remote chunk of the Italian Riviera, is the traffic-free, lowbrow, underappreciated alternative to the French Riviera. There's not a museum in sight—just sun, sea, sand (well, pebbles), wine, and pure, unadulterated Italy. Enjoy the villages, swimming, hiking, and evening romance of one of God's great gifts to tourism. For a home base, choose among five *(cinque)* villages, each of which fills a ravine with a lazy hive of human activity—callused locals, sunburned travelers, and no Vespas. While the Cinque Terre is now discovered (and can be quite crowded midday, when tourist boats and cruise-ship excursions drop by), I've never seen happier, more relaxed tourists.

The chunk of coast was first described in medieval times as "the five lands." In the feudal era, this land was watched over by castles. Tiny communities grew up in their protective shadows, ready to run inside at the first hint of a Turkish Saracen pirate raid. Marauding pirates from North Africa were a persistent problem until about 1400. Many locals were kidnapped and ransomed or sold into slavery, and those who remained built fires on flat-roofed watchtowers to relay warnings—alerting the entire coast to imminent attacks. The last major raid was in 1545.

As the threat of pirates faded, the villages prospered, catching fish and cultivating grapes. Churches were enlarged with a growing population. But until the advent of tourism in this generation, the towns remained isolated. Even today, traditions survive, and each of the five villages comes with a distinct dialect and its own proud heritage.

Sadly, a few ugly, noisy Americans give tourism a bad name

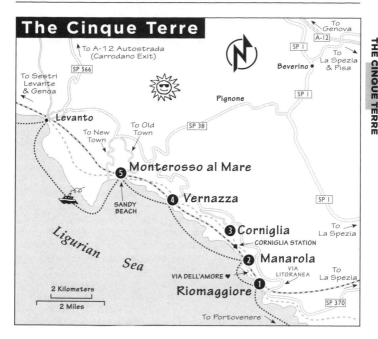

here. Even hip, young residents are put off by loud, drunken tourists. They say—and I agree—that the Cinque Terre is an exceptional place. It deserves a special dignity. Party in Viareggio or Portofino, but be mellow in the Cinque Terre. Talk softly. Help keep it clean. In spite of the tourist crowds, it's still a real community, and we are its guests.

In this chapter, I cover the five towns in order from south to north, from Riomaggiore to Monterosso. Since I still get the names of the towns mixed up, I think of them by number: #1 Riomaggiore (a workaday town), #2 Manarola (picturesque), #3 Corniglia (on a hilltop), #4 Vernazza (the region's cover girl, the most touristy and dramatic), and #5 Monterosso al Mare (the closest thing to a beach resort of the five towns).

Arrival in the Cinque Terre

By Train: Big, fast trains from elsewhere in Italy speed past the Cinque Terre (though some stop in Monterosso and Riomaggiore). Unless you're coming from a nearby town, you'll have to change trains at least once to reach Manarola, Corniglia, or Vernazza.

The Cinque Terre National Park— in Disarray

Since its creation in 1999, the Cinque Terre National Marine Park has brought plenty of good things to the area: money (visitors pay about €5 a day to hike the trails), new regulations to protect wildlife, and improved walkways, trails, beaches, breakwaters, and docks. Travelers have been able to take advantage of park-sponsored information centers and tiny folk museums.

The vision for the park was exciting—to have everyone thinking creatively about how to improve the area for the good of nature, the local communities, and their many visitors. The park administrators were well on their way to creating something unique in Europe. But, as so often happens in Italy, power and money corrupted the men entrusted to lead. Those working under them could see what was happening—but rather than try to stop the sleaze, many of them scrambled to get in on the easy money. The result is a vision gone completely out of focus and a park that's in disarray.

The park president, Franco Bonanini, was a powerful man—nicknamed "The Pharaoh" for his grandiose ideas. He initially impressed people as a visionary committed to the region and its precious park. But with a group of local bureaucrats—including Riomaggiore's mayor—he created a medieval-style system of favorites and enemies. This cabal was focused more on preserving their power than improving the park. As they started and stopped construction projects, funneling money here and there,

Generally, if you're coming from the north, you'll change trains in Sestri Levante or Genoa (specifically, Genoa's Piazza Principe station). If you're coming from the south or east, you'll most likely have to switch trains in La Spezia (change at La Spezia Centrale station—don't make the mistake of getting off at La Spezia Migliarina). No matter where you're coming from, it's best to check in the station before you leave to see your full schedule and route options (use the computerized kiosks or ask at a ticket window). Don't forget to validate your ticket by stamping it—ka-CHUNK!—in the yellow machines located on train platforms and elsewhere in the station. Conductors here are notorious for levying stiff fines on forgetful tourists. For more information on riding the train between Cinque Terre towns, see "Getting Around the Cinque Terre," later.

By Plane: If the Cinque Terre is your first, last, or only stop on this trip, consider flying into Pisa or Genoa, rather than Milan. These airports are less confusing than Milan's, and closer to the Cinque Terre.

By Car: If you're driving in the Cinque Terre (but, given the they derailed the park vision. In 2011, they were at last removed from power, but the damage had been done. Plans for future projects have been scuttled, and improvements already in place or underway—information offices, baggage deposits, mountain-biking opportunities, little museums, elevators for people with limited mobility, and even maintenance of the trails—have been abandoned.

Today, the park is run by a man from the central government whose plan, it seems, is to run the park as a business. But a park is a park, not a business. Ironically—and sadly, for the residents—using the park to wring money out of visitors while giving little back is not good for the livelihoods of the region's hardworking residents.

What does all this mean to the visitor? For 2012, no one knows exactly how the park will be functioning (for the latest, see www.parconazionale5terre.it). Otherwise, not much. The Cinque Terre is still my favorite chunk of Mediterranean coastline. Thankfully, the villages and dramatic stretches of land between them transcend any corrupt modern-day pharaohs. The people are endearing. The food, culture, and natural setting are uniquely enjoyable. But what's happened is disheartening. I thrill at the thought of people working together for a grand and noble vision that helps a community's economy by wisely treating a park as a park, rather than a moneymaker. And so far, the Cinque Terre has failed in that regard.

narrow roads and lack of parking, I wouldn't), see "Cinque Terre Connections" at the end of this chapter for directions.

Planning Your Time

The ideal stay is two or three full days; my recommended minimum stay is two nights and a completely uninterrupted day. The Cinque Terre is served by the local train from Genoa and La Spezia. Speed demons arrive in the morning, check their bags in La Spezia, take the five-hour hike through all five towns, laze away the afternoon on the beach or rock of their choice, and zoom away on the overnight train to somewhere back in the real world. But be warned: The Cinque Terre has a strange way of messing up your momentum. (The evidence is the number of Americans who have fallen in love with the region and/or one of its residents...and are still here.) Frankly, staying fewer than two nights is a mistake that you'll likely regret.

The towns are just a few minutes apart by hourly train or boat. There's no checklist of sights or experiences—just a hike, the towns themselves, and your fondest vacation desires. Study this chapter in advance and piece together your best day, mixing hiking, swimming, trains, and a boat ride. For the best light and coolest temperatures, start your hike early.

Market days perk up the towns from 8:00 to 13:00 on Tuesday in Vernazza, Wednesday in Levanto, Thursday in Monterosso and Sestri Levante, and Friday in La Spezia. (Levanto, Sestri Levante, and La Spezia are covered in the next chapter.)

The winter is really dead—most hotels and some restaurants close in December and January. The long Easter weekend (April 6-9 in 2012) and June and July are the peak of peak periods, the toughest times to find rooms. In spring, the towns can feel inundated with Italian school groups day-tripping on spring excursions (they can't afford to sleep in this expensive region).

For more information on the region, see www.cinqueterre.it.

Cinque Terre Park Cards

Visitors hiking between the towns need to pay a park entrance fee. This fee keeps the trails safe and open, and pays for viewpoints, picnic spots, WCs, and more. (Until recently, the fee also enriched corrupt local park managers—see the sidebar.) The popular coastal trail generates enough revenue to subsidize the development of trails and outdoor activities higher in the hills.

You have two options for covering the park fee: the Cinque Terre Park Card or the Cinque Terre Treno Park Card. Both are valid until midnight on the expiration date. Write your name on your card or risk a big fine.

The **Cinque Terre Park Card** costs €5 for one day of hiking or €9 for two (covers trails and shuttle buses but not trains, buy at trailheads and at most train stations, no validation required).

The **Cinque Terre Treno Park Card** covers what the Cinque Terre Park Card does, plus the use of the local trains (from Levanto to La Spezia, including all Cinque Terre towns). It's sold at TIs inside train stations, but not at trailheads (€10/1 day, €19/2 days, validate card at train station by punching it in the yellow machine). With this card, you have to hike and take three train trips every day just to break even.

Cards cost a bit more on weekends. Those under 18 or over 70 get a discount, as do families of four or more (see www.parco nazionale5terre.it).

Getting Around the Cinque Terre

Within the Cinque Terre, you can connect towns in three ways: by train, boat, or foot. Trains are cheaper, boats are more scenic, and hiking lets you enjoy more pasta. From a practical point of view, you should consider supplementing the often frustrating train with the sometimes more convenient boat. The trail between Riomaggiore and Manarola is a delight and takes just a few minutes, making the train not worth waiting for. The trail from Manarola to Corniglia is likely closed through much of 2012 (after a huge 2011 landslide).

By Train

Along the coast here, trains go in only two directions: *"per* [to] *Genova"* (the Italian spelling of Genoa), northbound; or *"per La*

Spezia," southbound. Assuming you're on vacation, accept the unpredictability of Cinque Terre trains (they're often late...unless you are, too—in which case they're on time). Relax while you wait—buy a cup of coffee at a station bar. When the train comes (know which direction to look for: La Spezia or Genova), casually walk over and hop on. This is especially easy in Monterosso, with its fine café-with-a-view on track #1 (direction: Milano/Genova), and in Vernazza, where you can hang out at the Blue Marlin Bar with a prepaid drink and dash when the train pulls in.

Use the handy TV monitors in the station, which display upcoming departures for the next hour or so (as well as notes about which track they're on and whether they're late). Most of the northbound trains that stop at all Cinque Terre towns and are headed toward Genova will list Sestri Levante as the *destinazione.*

By train, the five towns are just a few minutes apart. Know your stop. Once the train leaves the town just before your destination, go to the door and get ready to slip out before the mobs flood in, making it impossible to get off. Words to the wise for novice tourists, who often miss their stop: The stations are small and the trains are long, so (especially in Vernazza) you might have to get off deep in a tunnel. Also, the doors don't open automatically— you may have to flip open the handle of the door yourself. If a door isn't working, go quickly to the next car to leave. (When leaving a town by train, if you find the platform jammed with people, walk down the platform into the tunnel, where things quiet down.)

It costs about €1.80 per ride within the region. Tickets are good for 75 minutes in one direction, so you could conceivably use one for a brief stopover. To make the ticket good for six hours (in one direction only), you need to buy a ticket good for 40 kilometers (€3.50). Stamp the ticket at the station machine before you board. Machines are often broken or out of ink (good luck explaining that to conductors), but riding without a validated ticket can be expensive ("minimum €25 fine" means they charge what they want—usually €50). If you have a Eurailpass, don't spend one of your valuable flexi-days on the cheap Cinque Terre.

Events in the Cinque Terre in 2012

For more festival information, check www.cinqueterre.it and www.turismoinliguria.it. The food festivals in particular are subject to change.

April 8-9	All towns: Easter Sunday and Monday
April 25	All towns: Liberation Day (stay away from the Cinque Terre this day, as locals literally shut down the trails)
May 1	All towns: Labor Day (another local holiday that packs the place)
Mid-May	Monterosso: Lemon Festival (usually the third Sunday)
May 17	All towns: Ascension Day
June 7	Monterosso: Feast of Corpus Domini (procession on carpet of flowers at 18:00)
Mid-June	Monterosso: Anchovy Festival
June 24	Riomaggiore and Monterosso: Feast day of St. John the Baptist (procession and fireworks; big fire on Monterosso's old town beach the day before)
June 29	Corniglia: Feast day of Sts. Peter and Paul
July 20	Vernazza: Feast day of patron saint, St. Margaret, with fireworks
Aug 10	Manarola: Feast day of patron saint, St. Lawrence
Aug 14	Monterosso: Fireworks on eve of feast of the Assumption
Aug 15	All towns: Feast of the Assumption (*Ferragosto*)
Mid-Sept	Monterosso: Anchovies and Olive Oil Festival (usually the second weekend)

Cinque Terre Train Schedule: Since the train is the Cinque Terre's lifeline, many shops and restaurants post the current schedule, and most hotels offer copies of it (one also comes with the Cinque Terre Park Card). But beware: The printed schedules can be misleading (half the listed departures don't go every day); the monitors in the stations are your best source of actual, current departure information. Note that fast trains leaving La Spezia zip right through the Cinque Terre; some stop only in Monterosso (town #5) and Riomaggiore (town #1). But any train that stops in Manarola, Corniglia, and Vernazza (towns #2, #3, and #4) will stop in all five towns (including the trains on the schedule below).

The times below are accurate as of this printing, but confirm schedules locally. These are the daily train times (a few do not run on Sunday; more trains are added in the busiest season, June-Sept):

Trains leave La Spezia Centrale for all or most of the Cinque Terre villages at 7:12, 8:12, 10:07, 11:10, 12:00, 13:17, 14:06, 15:10, 16:01, 17:05, 17:27, 18:06, 19:29, 20:18, 21:23, 23:07, and 00:50.

Going back to La Spezia, trains leave Monterosso at 6:20, 8:15, 9:29, 11:00, 11:58 12:19, 13:26, 14:20, 15:22, 16:15, 17:30, 18:18, 19:22, 20:15, 20:30, 21:32, 22:22, and 23:45 (these same trains depart Vernazza about four minutes later).

Again, convenient TV monitors posted at several places in each station clearly show exactly what times the next trains are leaving in each direction (and, if they're late, how late they are expected to be). I trust these monitors much more than my ability to read any printed schedule.

By Boat

From Easter through October, a daily boat service connects Monterosso, Vernazza, Manarola, Riomaggiore, and Portovenere.

Boats provide a scenic way to get from town to town and survey what you just hiked. And boats offer the only efficient way to visit the nearby resort of Portovenere (see next chapter; the alternative is a tedious train-bus connection via La Spezia). In peaceful weather, the boats can be more reliable than the trains, but if seas are rough, they don't run at all. Because the boats nose in and tourists have to gingerly disembark onto little more than a plank, even a small chop can cancel some or all of the stops.

I see the tour boats as a syringe, injecting each town with a boost of euros. The towns are addicted, and they shoot up hourly through the summer. (Between 10:00-15:00—especially on weekends—masses of gawkers unload from boats, tour buses, and cruise ships, inundating the villages and changing the feel of the region.)

Boats depart Monterosso about hourly (10:30-17:00), stopping at the Cinque Terre towns (except at Corniglia) and ending up an hour later in Portovenere. (Portovenere-Monterosso boats run 9:00-17:00.) The ticket price depends on the length of the boat ride (short hops-€4, longer hops-€8, five-town all-day pass-€16). Round-trip tickets are slightly cheaper than two one-way trips. You can buy tickets at little stands at each town's harbor (tel. 0187-732-987 and 0187-818-440). Another all-day boat pass for

€23 extends to Portovenere and includes a 40-minute scenic ride around three small islands (2/day). Boats are not covered by the Cinque Terre Park Card. Boat schedules are posted at docks, harbor bars, Cinque Terre park offices, and hotels (www.navigazione golfodeipoeti.it).

By Shuttle Bus

Shuttle buses connect each Cinque Terre town with its distant parking lot and various points in the hills (for example, a shuttle runs from Corniglia's train station to its hilltop town center). Note that these shuttle buses do not connect the towns with each other. Most rides cost €1.50 (and are covered by the Cinque Terre Park Card)—pick up bus schedules from TIs or note the times posted on bus doors and at bus stops. Some (but not all) departures from Vernazza, Manarola, and Riomaggiore go beyond the parking lots and high into the hills. Pay for a round-trip ride and just cruise both ways to soak in the scenery (round-trip 30-45 minutes).

Hiking the Cinque Terre

All five towns are connected by good trails, marked with red-and-white paint, white arrows, and some signs. You'll experience the area's best by hiking all the way from one end to the other (although, unfortunately, the Manarola-Corniglia stretch is likely closed in 2012). While you can detour to dramatic hilltop sanctuaries, I'd keep it simple by following trail #2—the low route between the villages. The entire seven-mile hike can be

done in about four hours, but allow five for dawdling. Germans (with their task-oriented *Alpenstock* walking sticks) are notorious for marching too fast through the region. Take it slow...smell the cactus flowers and herbs, notice the lizards, listen to birds singing in the olive groves, and enjoy vistas on all sides.

Trails can be closed in bad weather or because of landslides. Remember that hikers need to pay a fee to enter the trails (see "Cinque Terre Park Cards," earlier). If you're hiking the entire five-town route, consider that the trail between Riomaggiore (#1) and Manarola (#2) is easiest. The hike between Manarola and Corniglia (#3) has minor hills (and is likely closed in 2012). The trail from Corniglia to Vernazza (#4) is demanding, and the path from Vernazza to Monterosso (#5) is the most challenging. For that hike, you might want to start in Monterosso in order to tackle the toughest section while you're fresh—and to enjoy the region's most dramatic scenery as you approach Vernazza.

Other than the wide, easy Riomaggiore-Manarola segment, the trail is generally narrow, steep, rocky, and comes with lots of steps. Be warned that I get many emails from readers who say the trail was tougher than they expected. The rocks and metal grates can be slippery in the rain. While the trail is a bit of a challenge, it's perfectly doable for any fit hiker...and worth the sweat.

Maps aren't necessary for the basic coastal hikes described here. But for the expanded version of this hike (12 hours, from Portovenere to Levanto) and more serious hikes in the high country, pick up a good hiking map (about €5, sold everywhere). To leave the park cleaner than you found it, bring a plastic bag *(sacchetto di plastica)* and pick up a little trail trash along the way. It would be great if American visitors—who get so much joy out of this region—were known for this good deed.

Riomaggiore-Manarola (20 minutes): Facing the front of the train station in Riomaggiore (#1), go up the stairs to the

right, following signs for *Via dell'Amore.* The photo-worthy promenade—wide enough for baby strollers—winds along the coast to Manarola (#2). It's primarily flat, and it's even wheelchair-accessible since there are elevators at each end (elevators at Riomaggiore included in pass, elevator at Manarola for disabled use only). While there's no beach along the trail, stairs lead down to sunbathing rocks. A long tunnel and mega-nets protect hikers from mean-spirited falling rocks. A wine bar—Bar & Vini A Piè de Mà—is located at the Riomaggiore trailhead and offers light meals, awesome town views, and clever boat storage under the train tracks. There's a picnic zone with a water fountain, shade, and a seagull that must have been human in a previous life hanging out just above the Manarola station (WC at Manarola station).

Manarola-Corniglia (45 minutes, likely closed in 2012): The walk from Manarola (#2) to Corniglia (#3) is a little longer, more rugged, and steeper than the Via dell'Amore. It's also less romantic. To avoid the last stretch (switchback stairs leading up to the hill-capping town of Corniglia), end your hike at Corniglia's train station and catch the shuttle bus to the town center (2/hour, €1.50, free with Cinque Terre Park Card, usually timed to meet the trains).

Corniglia-Vernazza (1.5 hours): The hike from Corniglia (#3) to Vernazza (#4)—the wildest and greenest section of the coast—is very rewarding but very hilly (going the other direction, from

Via dell'Amore

The Cinque Terre towns were extremely isolated until the last century. Villagers rarely married anyone from outside their town. After the blasting of a second train line in the 1920s, a trail was made between the first two towns: Riomaggiore and Manarola. The gunpowder warehouses built on each end, safely away from the townspeople, house cute little bars today.

Happy with the trail, the villagers asked that it be improved as a permanent connection between neighbors. But persistent landslides kept the trail closed more often than it was open. After World War II, the trail was reopened, and became established as a lovers' meeting point for boys and girls from the two towns. (After one extended closure in 1949, the trail was reopened for a Christmas marriage.) A journalist, who noticed all the amorous graffiti along the path, coined the trail's now-established name, Via dell'Amore: "Pathway of Love."

This new lane changed the social dynamics between the two villages, and made life much more fun and interesting for courting couples. Today, many tourists are put off by the cluttered graffiti that lines the trail. But it's all part of the history of the Cinque Terre's little lovers' lane.

You'll see padlocks locked to wires, cables, and fences. Closing a padlock with your lover at a lovey-dovey spot—often a bridge—is a common ritual in Italy (it was re-popularized by a teen novel a few years ago). In case you're so inclined, the hardware store next to Bar Centrale in Riomaggiore sells these locks. (You'll notice many of the locks come with the park logo.)

Major construction work—including the addition in 1994 of tunnels—has made the trail safer and keeps it open permanently. Notice how the brick-lined arcades match the train tunnel below. Rock-climbers from the north ("Dolomite spiders") were imported to help with the treacherous construction work. As you hike, look up and notice the massive steel netting bolted to the cliffside. Look down at the boulders that fell before the nets were added, and up at the boulders that have been caught...and be thankful for those Dolomite spiders.

Continuing the romance theme, benches along the way are named for lovers from Greek mythology. The many agave plants sport carved love notes—etched by amorous couples who likely don't know that the plant, which flowers once and then dies, is named for a tragic Greek story.

Vernazza to Corniglia, is steeper). From the Corniglia station and beach, zigzag up to the town (via the steep stairs, the longer road, or the shuttle bus). Ten minutes past Corniglia, toward Vernazza, you'll see Guvano beach far beneath you (once the region's nude beach). The scenic trail leads past a bar and picnic tables, through lots of fragrant and flowery vegetation, into Vernazza. If you need a break before reaching Vernazza, stop by Franco's Ristorante and Bar la Torre; it has a small menu but big views.

Vernazza-Monterosso (1.5 hours): The trail from Vernazza (#4) to Monterosso (#5) is a scenic up-and-down-a-lot trek and the most challenging of the bunch. Trails are narrow, steep, and crumbly, with a lot of steps (some readers report "very dangerous"), but easy to follow. Locals frown on camping at the picnic tables located midway. The views just out of Vernazza, looking back at the town, are spectacular.

Longer Hikes: Above the trails that run between the towns, higher-elevation hikes crisscross the region. Shuttle buses make the going easier, connecting coastal villages and trailheads in the hills. Ask locally about the more difficult six-mile inland hike to Volastra. This tiny village, perched between Manarola and Corniglia, hosts lots of Germans and Italians in the summertime. Just below its town center, in the hamlet of Groppo, is the Cinque Terre Cooperative Winery (open daily). For the whole trip on the high road between Manarola and Corniglia, allow two hours one-way. In return, you'll get sweeping views and a closer look at the vineyards. Shuttle buses run from Manarola to Volastra (€2.50 or free with Cinque Terre Park Card, pick up schedule from park office, 8/day, more departures in summer, 15 minutes); consider taking the bus up and hiking down.

Swimming, Kayaking, and Biking

Every town in the Cinque Terre has a beach or a rocky place to swim. Monterosso has the biggest and sandiest beach, with umbrellas and beach-use fees (but it's free where there are no umbrellas). Vernazza's is tiny—better for sunning than swimming. Manarola and Riomaggiore have the worst beaches (no sand), but Manarola offers the best deep-water swimming.

Wear your walking shoes and pack your swim gear. Several of the beaches have showers (no shampoo, please). Underwater sightseeing is full of fish—goggles are sold in local shops. Sea urchins can be a problem if you walk on the rocks, and sometimes jellyfish wash up on the pebbles.

You can rent kayaks or boats in Riomaggiore, Vernazza, and Monterosso. (For details, see individual town listings in this chapter.) Some readers say kayaking can be dangerous—the kayaks tip easily, training is not provided, and lifejackets are not required.

Sleeping in the Cinque Terre

If you think too many people have my book, avoid Vernazza. You get fewer crowds and better value for your money in other towns. Monterosso is a good choice for sun-worshipping softies, those who prefer the ease of a real hotel, and the younger crowd (more nightlife). Hermits, anarchists, wine-lovers, and mountain goats like Corniglia. Sophisticated Italians and Germans choose Manarola. Riomaggiore is bigger than Vernazza and less resorty than Monterosso.

While the Cinque Terre is too rugged for the mobs that ravage the Spanish and French coasts, it's popular with Italians, Germans, and in-the-know Americans. Hotels charge more and are packed on holidays (including Easter); in June, July, and September; and on Fridays and Saturdays all summer. (With global warming, sweltering August is no longer considered peak season on this stretch of the Riviera.) While you can find doubles for €65 or €70 most of the season, you'll pay extra (around €80) in June and July. The prices I've listed are the maximum for April through October. For a terrace or view, you might pay an extra €20 or more. Apartments for four can be economical for families—figure around €120.

It's smart to reserve your room in advance in May, June, July, and September, and on weekends and holidays. At other times,

you can land a double room on any day by just arriving in town (ideally by noon) and asking around at bars and restaurants, or simply by approaching locals on the street. Many travelers enjoy the opportunity to shop around a bit and get the best price by bargaining. Private rooms—called *affitta camere*—are no longer an intimate stay with a family. They are generally comfortable apartments (often with small kitchens) where you get the key and come and go as you like, rarely seeing your landlord. Many landowners rent the buildings by the year to local managers, who then attempt to make a profit by filling them night after night with tourists.

For the best value, visit several private rooms and snare the best. Going direct cuts out the middleman and softens prices. Staying more than one night gives you bargaining leverage. Plan on paying cash. Private rooms are generally bigger and more comfortable than those offered by pensions and have the same privacy as a hotel room.

If you want the security of a reservation, make it at a hotel long in advance (smaller places generally don't take reservations very far ahead). Query by email, not fax. If you do reserve, honor your reservation (or, if you must cancel, do it as early as possible). Since people renting rooms usually don't take deposits, they lose money if you don't show up.

Eating in the Cinque Terre

Hanging out at a sea-view restaurant while sampling local specialties could become one of your favorite memories.

Tegame alla Vernazza is the most typical main course in Vernazza: anchovies, potatoes, tomatoes, white wine, oil, and herbs. Anchovies (*acciughe*; ah-CHOO-gay) are ideally served the day they're caught. There's nothing cool about being an anchovy virgin. If you've always hated anchovies (the harsh, cured-in-salt American kind), try them fresh here. *Pansotti* are ravioli with ricotta and a mixture of greens, often served with a walnut sauce... delightful and filling.

While antipasto means cheese and salami in Tuscany, here you'll get *antipasti frutti di mare*, a plate of mixed "fruits of the sea" and a fine way to start a meal. Many restaurants are particularly proud of their *antipasti frutti di mare*. For two diners, splitting one of these and a pasta dish can be plenty.

This region is the birthplace of pesto. Basil, which loves the temperate Ligurian climate, is ground with cheese (half parmigiano cow cheese and half pecorino sheep cheese), garlic, olive oil, and pine nuts, and then poured over pasta. Try it on spaghetti, *trenette* (the long, flat Ligurian noodle), or *trofie* (made of flour with a bit of potato, designed specifically for pesto to cling to). Many also like pesto lasagna, always made with white sauce, never red. If you become addicted, small jars of pesto are sold in the local grocery stores and gift shops. If it's refrigerated, it's fresh; this is what you want if you're eating it today. For taking home, get the jar-on-a-shelf pesto.

Focaccia, the tasty pillowy bread, also originates here in Liguria. Locals say the best focaccia is made between the Cinque Terre and Genoa. It's simply flatbread with olive oil and salt. The baker roughs up the dough with finger holes, then bakes it. Focaccia comes plain or with onions, sage, or olive bits, and is a local favorite for a snack on the beach. Bakeries sell it in rounds or slices by the weight (a portion is about 100 grams, or *un etto*).

Farinata, a humble fried bread snack, is made from chickpea meal, water, oil, and pepper, and baked on a copper tray in a wood-burning stove. *Farinata* is sold at pizza and focaccia places.

The *vino delle Cinque Terre*, while not one of Italy's top wines, flows cheap and easy throughout the region. It's white—great with seafood. For a sweet dessert wine, the *sciacchetrà* wine is worth the splurge (€4 per small glass, often served with a cookie). You could order the fun dessert *torta della nonna* (grandmother's cake) and dunk chunks of it into your glass. Aged *sciacchetrà* is dry and costly (up to €12/glass). While 10 kilos of grapes yield seven liters of local wine, *sciacchetrà* is made from near-raisins, and 10 kilos of grapes make only 1.5 liters of *sciacchetrà*. The word means "push and pull"—push in lots of grapes, pull out the best wine. If your room is up a lot of steps, be warned: *Sciacchetrà* is 18 percent alcohol, while regular wine is only 11 percent.

In the cool, calm evening, sit on Vernazza's breakwater with a glass of wine and watch the phosphorescence in the waves.

Nightlife in the Cinque Terre

While the Cinque Terre is certainly not noted for bumping beach-town nightlife like nearby Viareggio, you'll find some sort of travel-tale-telling hub in Monterosso, Vernazza, and Riomaggiore (Manarola and Corniglia are sleepy). Monterosso has a lively scene, especially in the summertime—but no *discoteca* yet. In Vernazza, the nightlife centers in the bars on the waterfront piazza, which is the small-town-style place to "see and be seen." A town law requires all bars to shut by midnight. Bar Centrale in Riomaggiore is, well, the central place for cocktails and meeting fellow travelers. (For details, see the "Nightlife" sections for these three villages.) Wherever your night adventures take you, have fun, but please remember that residents live upstairs.

Helpful Hints for the Cinque Terre

Tourist and Park Information: Each town (except Corniglia) has a well-staffed TI and park office (listed throughout this chapter).

Money: Banks and ATMs are plentiful throughout the region.

Baggage Storage: You can store bags at La Spezia's train station (€3/12 hours, 8:00-22:00) and at Lucia's Lavarapido in Monterosso (€5/day).

Services: Every train station has a handy public WC. Otherwise, pop into a bar or restaurant.

Taxi: Cinqueterre Taxi covers all five towns (mobile 328-583-4969, www.cinqueterretaxi.com, info@cinqueterretaxi.com).

Local Guides: Andrea Bordigoni is both knowledgeable and a delight (€110/half-day, €175/day, mobile 347-972-3317, bordigo @inwind.it). Other local guides are **Marco Brizzi** (mobile 328-694-2847, marco_brizzi@yahoo.it) and **Paola Tommarchi** (paolatomma@alice.it).

Booking Agency: Miriana and Filippo at **Cinque Terre Riviera** book rooms in the Cinque Terre towns, Portovenere, and La Spezia for a 10 percent markup over the list price (can also arrange transportation, cooking classes, and weddings; Via Picedi 18 in La Spezia; tel. 0187-520-702, Miriana—mobile

340-794-7358, Filippo—mobile 393-939-1901, www.cinque terreriviera.com, info@cinqueterreriviera.com, English spoken).

Riomaggiore (Town #1)

The most substantial non-resort town of the group, Riomaggiore is a disappointment from the train station. But once you leave that neighborhood, you'll discover a fascinating tangle of pastel homes leaning on each other like drunken sailors. Just walk through the tunnel next to the train tracks, and you'll discover a more real, laid-back, and workaday town than its touristy neighbors.

Orientation to Riomaggiore

Tourist Information
The TI is in the train station at the ticket desk (daily 8:00-18:00, tel. 0187-920-633). If the TI in the station is crowded, buy your hiking pass at the Cinque Terre park shop/information office next door by the mural (daily 8:00-19:30, tel. 0187-760-515, netpoint riomaggiore@parconazionale5terre.it).

For an informal information source, try Ivo and Alberto, who run Bar Centrale (see "Nightlife in Riomaggiore," later).

Arrival in Riomaggiore
The bus shuttles locals and tourists up and down Riomaggiore's steep main street and continues to the parking lot outside town (€1.50 one-way, €2.50 round-trip, free with Cinque Terre Park Card, 2/hour but almost comically erratic, main stop at the fork of Via Colombo and Via Malborghetto, or flag it down as it passes).

Helpful Hints
Internet Access: The **park shop/information office** has eight Internet terminals upstairs and Wi-Fi (€0.08/minute, daily May-Sept 8:00-22:00, Oct-April until 19:30). **Hotel la Zorza** has several terminals in town and charges about the same (daily 11:00-21:30, under the archway just past the Co-op grocery store). **Bar Centrale** offers free Wi-Fi with the purchase of a drink (see "Nightlife in Riomaggiore," later).
Laundry: A self-service launderette is on the main street (€3.50/

To Manarola

VIA DELL'AMORE **TRAIN STATION**

Cliffs

MURALS

16

CINQUE TERRE INFO

ELEVATOR TO HIGH ROAD

13

VIA PECUNIA

VIA SIGNORINI

VIA

PEDESTRIAN TUNNEL

VIA SANT'ANTONIO

PUNTA

9

Cliffs

10

12

VIA SAN GIACOMO

BOAT DOCK

Harbor

BREAKWATER

BOAT TICKETS

Ligurian Sea

❶ Locanda del Sole
❷ Locanda Ca' dei Duxi
❸ Hotel la Zorza
❹ Locanda dalla Compagnia
❺ Riomaggiore Reservations
❻ La Dolce Vita Rooms
❼ Edi's Rooms & Launderette
❽ Camere Patrizia
❾ Trattoria la Grotta
❿ La Lanterna Ristorante
⓫ Te la Do Io la Merenda Snack Bar
⓬ Enoteca & Ristorante Dau Cila
⓭ Bar & Vini A Piè de Mà
⓮ Bar Centrale & Gelateria
⓯ Madonna di Montenero Trail
⓰ Park Office Kiosk

wash, €3.50/dry, daily 8:30-20:00, run by Edi's Rooms next door, Via Colombo 111).

Self-Guided Walk

Welcome to Riomaggiore

Here's an easy loop trip that maximizes views and minimizes uphill walking.

• *Start at the train station. (If you arrive by boat, cross beneath the tracks and take a left, then hike through the tunnel along the tracks to reach the station.) You'll come to some...*

Colorful Murals: These murals, with subjects modeled after real-life Riomaggiorians, glorify the nameless workers who constructed the nearly 300 million cubic feet of dry-stone walls (without cement) that run

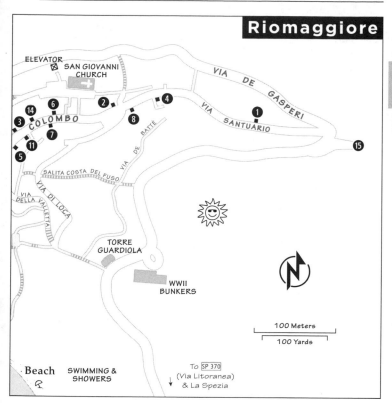

throughout the Cinque Terre. These walls give the region its characteristic *muri a secco* terracing for vineyards and olive groves. The
murals, done by Argentinean artist Silvio Benedetto, are well-
explained in English.

• *Head to the railway tunnel entrance, and ride the elevator to the top
of town (€0.50 or €1 family ticket, free with Cinque Terre Park Card,
daily 8:00-19:45). If the elevator is closed (likely), hike around to the
left, following the road up and then right to the...*

Top o' the Town: Here you're treated to spectacular sea views.
To continue the viewfest, go right and follow the walkway (ignore
the steps marked *Marina Seacoast* that lead to the harbor). It's a
five-minute level stroll to the church. You'll pass under the offices
of the disgraced national park president and the city hall (flying
two flags), with murals celebrating the heroic grape-pickers and
fishermen of the region (also by Silvio Benedetto).

• *Before reaching the church, pause to enjoy the...*

Town View: The major river of this region once ran through
this valley, as implied by the name Riomaggiore (local dialect for
"river" and "major"). As in the other Cinque Terre towns, the river

ravine is now paved over, and the romantic arched bridges that once connected the two sides have been replaced by a practical modern road.

Notice the lack of ugly aerial antennae. In the 1980s, every residence got cable. Now, the TV tower on the hilltop behind the church steeple brings the modern world into each home. The church was rebuilt in 1870, but was first established in 1340. It's dedicated to St. John the Baptist, the patron saint of Genoa, the maritime republic that once dominated the region. The elevator next to the church may be completed by the time you get here. It's designed to help seniors get around the steep town, and also to link to the elevator near the Via dell'Amore trailhead.

• *Continue past the church down to Riomaggiore's main street, named...*

Via Colombo: Walk about 30 feet beyond the WC, go down the stairs, and—if it's open—pop into the tiny Cinque Terre Antiche museum (€0.50, free with Cinque Terre Park Card, generally closed). Sit down for a few minutes to watch a circa-1950 video of the Cinque Terre.

Continuing down Via Colombo, you'll pass a bakery, a couple of grocery shops, and the self-service laundry. There's homemade gelato next to the Bar Centrale. Above where Via Colombo dead-ends, a park-like square built over the train tracks gives the children of the town a level bit of land upon which to kick their soccer balls. The murals above celebrate the great-grandparents of these very children—the salt-of-the-earth locals who earned a humble living before the age of tourism. To the left, stairs lead down to the Marina neighborhood, with the harbor, the boat dock, a 200-yard trail to the beach *(spiaggia),* and an inviting little art gallery. To the right of the stairs is the pedestrian tunnel, running alongside the tracks, which takes you directly back to the station and the trail to the other towns. From here, you can take a train, hop a boat, or hike to your next destination.

Sights in Riomaggiore

Beach—Riomaggiore's rugged and tiny "beach" is rocky, but it's clean and peaceful. Take a two-minute walk from the harbor: Face the harbor, then follow the path to your left. Passing the rugged boat landing, stay on the path to the pebbly beach. There's a shower there in the summer, and another closer to town by the boat landing—where many enjoying sunning on and jumping from the rocks.

Kayaks and Water Sports—The town has a diving center (scuba, snorkeling, kayaks; office down the stairs and under the tracks on Via San Giacomo, daily May-Sept 9:00-18:00, tel. 0187-920-011, www.5terrediving.it).

Hikes—The cliff-hanging Torre Guardiola trail, a steep 20-minute climb from the beach up to old WWII bunkers and a hilltop botanical pathway, has been closed because of a rock slide. Another trail rises from Riomaggiore scenically to the 14th-century Madonna di Montenero sanctuary, high above the town (45 minutes, take the main road inland until you see signs, or ride the green shuttle bus 12 minutes from the town center to the sanctuary trail, then walk uphill 10 minutes).

Nightlife in Riomaggiore

Bar Centrale, run by sociable Ivo, Alberto, and the gang, offers "nightlife" any time of day—making it a good stop for Italian breakfast and music. Ivo, who lived in San Francisco, fills his bar with San Franciscan rock and a fun-loving vibe. During the day, this is a shaded place to relax with other travelers. At night, it offers the younger set the liveliest action (and best mojitos) in town. They also serve €5 fast-food pastas and microwaved pizzas (daily 7:30-24:00 or later, closed Mon in winter, free Wi-Fi with drink, in the town center at Via Colombo 144, tel. 0187-920-208). There's a good *gelateria* next door.

Enoteca & Ristorante Dau Cila, a cool little hideaway with a mellow jazz-and-Brazilian-lounge ambience down at the miniscule harbor, is a counterpoint to wild Bar Centrale. It's cool for cocktails and open nightly until 24:00 (snacks and meals, fine wine by the glass; see "Eating in Riomaggiore," later).

Bar & Vini A Piè de Mà, at the beginning of Via dell'Amore, has piles of charm, €6 cocktails, often music, and stays open until midnight June through September (see "Eating in Riomaggiore," later).

The marvelous **Via dell'Amore** trail (described earlier), lit only with subtle ground lighting so that you can see the stars, welcomes romantics after dark. The trail is free after 19:30.

Sleeping in Riomaggiore

Riomaggiore has arranged its private-room rental system better than its neighbors. Several agencies—with regular office hours, English-speaking staff, and email addresses—line up within a few yards of each other on the main drag. Each manages a corral of local rooms for rent. These offices keep erratic hours, so it's smart to settle up the day before you leave in case they're closed when you need to depart. Expect lots of stairs. If you don't mind the hike, the street above town has safe overnight parking (free 20:00-8:00).

Sleep Code

(€1 = about $1.40, country code: 39)
S = Single, **D** = Double/Twin, **T** = Triple, **Q** = Quad, **b** = bathroom, **s** = shower only. Unless otherwise noted, credit cards are accepted, English is spoken, and breakfast is included (except in Vernazza).

To help you sort easily through these listings, I've divided the accommodations into three categories based on the price for a standard double room with bath:

$$$ Higher Priced—Most rooms €100 or more.
  $$ Moderately Priced—Most rooms between €50-100.
    $ Lower Priced—Most rooms €50 or less.

Prices can change without notice; verify the hotel's current rates online or by email. For other updates, see www .ricksteves.com/update.

Hotels

$$$ Locanda del Sole has seven modern, basic, and overpriced rooms with a shared and peaceful terrace. Located at the utilitarian top end of town, it's a five-minute walk downhill to the center. Easy (and free with this book) parking makes it especially appealing to drivers (Db-€110-120, air-con, Wi-Fi, Via Santuario 114, tel. & fax 0187-920-773, mobile 340-983-0090, www.locandadel sole.net, info@locandadelsole.net, Enrico).

$$$ Locanda Ca' dei Duxi rents 10 good rooms from an efficient little office on the main drag (Db-€100-130 depending on view and season, extra person-€20, air-con, Wi-Fi, parking-€10/day—book when you reserve, open year-round, Via Colombo 36, tel. & fax 0187-920-036, mobile 329-825-7836, www.duxi.it, info @duxi.it, Samuele and Anna). They also manage **Ca' dei Lisci,** with simpler and cheaper rooms (D-€60, Db-€70-80, www.cadei lisci.com).

$$$ Hotel la Zorza rents nine decent but overpriced rooms in the tangled lanes in the center of town (Db-€100-130, Qb apartment-€150, air-con, Wi-Fi, Via Colombo 36, tel. & fax 0187-920-036, mobile 329-825-7836, www.hotelzorza.com, info@duxi.it).

$$ Locanda dalla Compagnia rents five modern rooms at the top of town, just 300 yards below the parking lot and the little church. All rooms—nice but rather dim—are on the same tranquil ground floor, and share an inviting lounge. Franca runs it with the help of son Allessandro (Db-€80, cash only, air-con, mini-fridge, no view, Via del Santuario 232, tel. 0187-760-050, fax 0187-920-586, www.dallacompagnia.it, lacomp@libero.it).

Room-Booking Services

$$ Riomaggiore Reservations offers 12 rooms and 15 apartments, with American expats Amy and Maddy smoothing communications (Db-€60-90 depending on view, Db suite with top view-€120, cash only, reception open 9:00-17:00 in season, Via Colombo 181, tel. & fax 0187-760-575, www.riomaggiorereservations.com, info@riomaggiorereservations.com).

$$ La Dolce Vita offers three fine rooms on the main drag and two apartments around town (Db-€60-80, open daily 9:30-19:30; if they're closed, they're full; Via Colombo 120, tel. 0187-760-044, mobile 329-099-2741, agonatal@interfree.it, helpful Giacomo and Simone).

$$ Edi's Rooms rents 20 rooms and apartments. You pay extra for views (Db-€70-90 depending on room, apartment Qb-€100-160, reserve with credit card, office open daily in summer 8:30-20:00, in winter 10:30-12:30 & 14:30-19:00, some rooms involve climbing a lot of steps—ask before viewing or reserving, reception at Via Colombo 111, tel. 0187-760-842, tel. & fax 0187-920-325, www.lancoracinqueterre.com, edi-vesigna@iol.it).

Backpacker Dorms

$ Riomaggiore Reservations (listed above) runs a mini-hostel in a fine communal apartment with nine beds in three rooms, a cool living room, terrace, and kitchen in a good, quiet location. Take care of this little treasure so it survives (€22/bed, reception open 9:00-17:00 in season, Via Colombo 181, tel. & fax 0187-760-575, www.riomaggiorereservations.com, info@riomaggiorereservations.com).

$ Camere Patrizia rents cheap doubles and dorm bunk beds at €25 per person from its reception at Via Colombo 25, but books only through www.hostelworld.com or to drop-ins (mobile 333-165-6362).

Eating in Riomaggiore

Trattoria La Grotta, right in the town center (no view), serves reliably good food with a passion for anchovies and mussels. You'll enjoy friendly service surrounded by historic photos and wonderful stonework in a dramatic, dressy, cave-like setting. Venessa is warm and helpful while her mother, Isa, is busy cooking (€12 pastas, €15 *secondi*, 5 percent cash discount, Thu-Tue 12:00-14:30 & 17:30-22:30, closed Wed, Via Colombo 247, tel. 0187-920-187).

La Lanterna, with the ambience of an old fisherman's home inside and a few appealing harborside tables outside, is wedged into a niche in the Marina, overlooking the harbor under the tracks. Chef Massimo serves traditional plates, loves anchovies, and bakes fresh bread daily (€10 pastas, €18 *secondi*, no cover, daily 12:00-22:00, Via San Giacomo 10, tel. 0187-920-589).

Te La Do Io La Merenda ("I'll Give You a Snack") is good for a snack, pizza, or takeout. Their counter is piled with an assortment of munchies, and they have pastas, roasted chicken, and focaccia sandwiches to go (daily 9:00-21:00, Via Colombo 161, tel. 0187-920-148).

Enoteca & Ristorante Dau Cila is decked out like a black-and-white movie set in a centuries-old boat shed with extra tables outside on a rustic deck over dinghies. Try their antipasto specialty of several seafood appetizers, and listen to jazz with the waves lapping at the harbor below (€12 pastas, €18 *secondi*, March-Oct daily until 24:00, Via San Giacomo 65, tel. 0187-760-032, Luca).

Bar & Vini A Piè de Mà, at the trailhead on the Manarola end of town, is good for a scenic light bite or quiet drink at night. Enjoying a meal at a table on its dramatically situated terrace provides an indelible Cinque Terre memory (daily 10:00-20:00, June-Sept until 24:00, tel. 0187-921-037).

Picnics: Groceries and delis lining Via Colombo sell food to go, including pizza slices, for a picnic at the harbor or beach.

Manarola (Town #2)

Like Riomaggiore, Manarola is attached to its station by a 200-yard-long tunnel (lined with interesting photos). During WWII air raids, these tunnels provided refuge and a safe place for rattled villagers to sleep. The town itself fills a ravine, bookended by its wild little harbor to the west and a diminutive church square inland to the east. A delightful and gentle stroll from the church down to the harborside park provides the region's easiest vineyard walk (described in my "Self-Guided Walk," next page).

Orientation to Manarola

The **TI** at the train station is open daily 7:00-20:00.

A **shuttle bus** runs between the low end of Manarola's main street (at the tobacco shop and newsstand) and the parking lot (€1.50 one-way, €2.50 round-trip, free with Cinque Terre Park Card, 2/hour, just flag it down). Shuttle buses also run about hourly from Manarola to Volastra, near the Cinque Terre Cooperative Winery.

To get to the **dock** and the boats that connect Manarola with the other Cinque Terre towns, find the steps to the left of the harbor view—they lead down to the ticket kiosk. Continue around the left side of the cliff (as you're facing the water) to catch the boats.

Self-Guided Walk

Welcome to Manarola

From the harbor, this 30-minute circular walk shows you the town and surrounding vineyards, and ends at a fantastic viewpoint, perfect for a picnic.

• *Start down at the waterfront.*

The Harbor: Manarola is tiny and picturesque, a tumble of buildings bunny-hopping down its ravine to the fun-loving waterfront. Notice how the I-beam crane launches the boats. Facing the water, look to the right, at the hillside Punta Bonfiglio cemetery and park (where this walk ends).

The town's swimming hole is just below. Manarola has no sand, but offers the best deep-water swimming in the area. The first "beach" has a shower, ladder, and wonderful rocks. The second has tougher access and no shower, but feels more remote and pristine (follow the paved path toward Corniglia, just around the point). For many, the tricky access makes this beach dangerous.

• *Hiking inland up the town's main drag, you'll come to the train tracks covered by Manarola's new square, called...*

Piazza Capellini: Built in 2004, this square is an all-around great idea, giving the town a safe, fun zone for kids. Locals living near the tracks also enjoy a little less noise. Check out the mosaic that displays the varieties of local fish in colorful enamel.

• *Fifty yards uphill, you'll find the...*

Sciacchetrà Museum: Run by the national park, it's hardly a museum. But if it's open, pop in to its inviting room to see a tiny exhibit on the local wine industry (€0.50, free with Cinque Terre Park Card, generally closed, 15-minute video in English by request, 100 yards uphill from train tracks, across from the post office).

• *Hiking farther uphill, you can still hear...*

Manarola's Stream: As in Riomaggiore, Monterosso, and

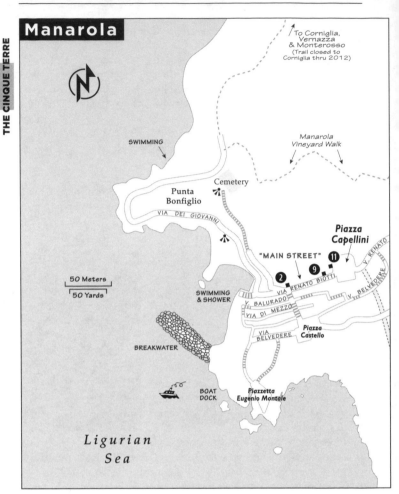

Vernazza, Manarola's stream was covered over by a modern sewage system after World War II. Before that time, romantic bridges arched over its ravine. A modern waterwheel recalls the origin of the town's name—local dialect for "big wheel" (one of many possible derivations). Mills like this once powered the local olive oil industry.

• *Keep climbing until you come to the square at the...*

Top of Manarola: The square is faced by a church, an oratory—now a religious and community meeting place—and a bell tower, which served as a watchtower when pirates raided the town (the cupola was added once the attacks ceased). Behind the church is Manarola's well-run youth hostel, originally the church's schoolhouse. To the right of the oratory, a stepped lane leads to

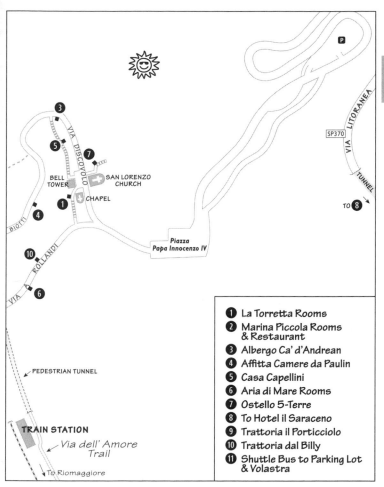

Legend:
1. La Torretta Rooms
2. Marina Piccola Rooms & Restaurant
3. Albergo Ca' d'Andrean
4. Affitta Camere da Paulin
5. Casa Capellini
6. Aria di Mare Rooms
7. Ostello 5-Terre
8. To Hotel il Saraceno
9. Trattoria il Porticciolo
10. Trattoria dal Billy
11. Shuttle Bus to Parking Lot & Volastra

Manarola's sizable tourist-free zone.

While you're here, check out the church. According to the white marble plaque in its facade, the Parish Church of St. Lawrence (San Lorenzo) dates from "MCCCXXXVIII" (1338). Step inside to see two paintings from the unnamed Master of the Cinque Terre, the only painter of any note from this region (left wall and above main altar). While the style is Gothic, the work dates from the late 15th century, long after Florence had entered the Renaissance. Note the humble painted stone ceiling, which replaced the wooden original in the 1800s. It features Lawrence, patron saint of the Cinque Terre, with his grill, the symbol of his martyrdom (he was roasted on it).

• *Walk 20 yards below the church and find a wooden railing. It marks the start of a delightful stroll around the high side of town, and back to the seafront. This is the beginning of the...*

Manarola Vineyard Walk: Don't miss this experience. Simply follow the wooden railing, enjoying lemon groves and wild red valerian (used for insomnia since the days of the Romans). Along the path, which is primarily flat, you'll get a close-up look at the region's famous dry-stone walls and finely crafted vineyards (with dried-heather thatches to protect the grapes from the southwest winds). Smell the rosemary. Study the structure of the town, and pick out the scant remains of an old fort. Notice the S-shape of the main road—once a riverbed—that flows through town. The town's roofs are traditionally made of locally quarried slate, rather than tile, and are held down by rocks during windstorms. As the harbor comes into view, you'll see the breakwater, added just a decade ago.

Out of sight above you on the right are simple wooden religious scenes, the work of local resident Mario Andreoli. Before his father died, Mario promised him he'd replace the old cross on the family's vineyard. Mario has been adding figures ever since. After recovering from a rare illness, he redoubled his efforts. On religious holidays, everything's lit up: the Nativity, the Last Supper, the Crucifixion, the Resurrection, and more. Some of the scenes are left up year-round.

High above, a recent fire burned off the tree cover, revealing ancient terraces that line the terrain like a topographic map.

• *Follow this trail all the way to a T-intersection, where it hits the main coastal trail. Turn left. (A right takes you to the trail to Corniglia, likely closed in 2012.) Before descending back into town, take a right, detouring into...*

The Cemetery: Ever since Napoleon—who was king of Italy in the early 1800s—decreed that cemeteries were health risks, Cinque Terre's burial spots have been located outside the towns. The result: The dearly departed generally get first-class sea views. Each cemetery—with its evocative yellowed photos and finely carved Carrara marble memorial reliefs—is worth a visit. (The basic structure for all of them is the same, but Manarola's is the most easily accessible.)

In cemeteries like these, there's a hierarchy of four places to park your mortal remains: a graveyard, a spacious death condo *(loculo)*, a mini bone-niche *(ossario)*, or the communal ossuary. Because of the tight space, a time limit is assigned to the first three options (although many older tombs are grandfathered in). Bones go into the ossuary in the middle of the chapel floor after about a generation. Traditionally, locals make weekly visits to loved ones here, often bringing flowers. The rolling stepladder makes access to top-floor *loculi* easy.

• *The Manarola cemetery is on Punta Bonfiglio. Walk just below it, far-*

ther out through a park (playground, drinking water, WC, and picnic benches). Your Manarola finale: the bench at the tip of the point, offering one of the most commanding views of the entire region. The easiest way back to town is to take the stairs at the end of the point.

Sleeping in Manarola

(€1 = about $1.40, country code: 39)

Manarola has plenty of private rooms. Ask in bars and restaurants. There's a modern three-star place halfway up the main drag, a sea-view hotel on the harbor, a big modern hostel, and a cluster of options around the church at the peaceful top of the town (a 5-minute hike from the train tracks).

$$$ **La Torretta** is a trendy, upscale 13-room place that caters to a demanding clientele. Probably the most elegant retreat in the region, it's a peaceful refuge with all the comforts for those happy to pay, including a communal hot tub with a view. Enjoy a complimentary snack and glass of prosecco on arrival, free wine-tastings during your stay, breakfast in your room, and a free minibar. Each chic room is distinct and described on their website (smaller Db-€145, regular Db-€190, Db suite-€250-400, 10 percent discount with cash, book several months in advance as it's justifiably popular, closed mid-Nov-mid-March, Wi-Fi, on Piazza della Chiesa beside the bell tower at Vico Volto 20, tel. 0187-920-327, fax 0187-760-024, www.torrettas.com, torretta@cdh.it).

$$$ **Marina Piccola** offers 13 bright, slick rooms on the water—so they figure a warm welcome is unnecessary (Db-€120, air-con, Wi-Fi, Via Birolli 120, tel. 0187-920-103, fax 0187-920-966, www.hotelmarinapiccola.com, info@hotelmarinapiccola.com).

$$$ **Albergo Ca' d'Andrean,** run by Simone, is quiet, comfortable, and modern—except for its antiquated reservation system. While the welcome is formal at best, it has 10 big, sunny, air-conditioned rooms and a cool garden oasis complete with lemon trees (Sb-€72, Db-€100, breakfast-€6, cash only, send personal check to reserve from US—or call if you're reserving from the road, closed Nov-Christmas, up the hill at Via A. Discovolo 101, tel. 0187-920-040, fax 0187-920-452, www.cadandrean.it, cadandrean@libero.it).

$$ At **Affitta Camere da Paulin,** charming Donatella and Eraldo (the town's retired policeman) rent very nice, well-equipped rooms with a large and inviting common living room. It's in a modern setting a few minutes' walk uphill from the train tracks (Db-€70-80, view apartment Db-€105-130, Wi-Fi, Via Discovolo 126, tel. & fax 0187-920-706, mobile 334-389-4764, www.dapaulin.it, prenotazioni@dapaulin.it).

$$ Casa Capellini rents four rooms: One has a view balcony, another a 360-degree terrace—book long in advance (Sb-€45, Db-€65; €85 for the *alta camera* on the top, with a kitchen, private terrace, and knockout view; two doors down the hill from the church—with your back to the church, it's at 2 o'clock; Via Ettore Cozzani 12, tel. 0187-920-823, mobile 349-306-1046, www .casacapellini-5terre.it, casa.capellini@tin.it, Gianni and Franca don't speak English).

$$ Aria di Mare Rooms rents four sunny rooms and an apartment 20 yards beyond Trattoria dal Billy at the very top of town. Three rooms have spacious terraces with knockout views and lounge chairs. Maurizio speaks a little English, while Mamma Franca communicates with lots of Italian and toothy smiles (Db-€80, 2 adults and 1 child-€80, Db apartment-€90, these prices promised through 2012, no breakfast, Wi-Fi, up stairs on the left at Via Aldo Rollandi 137, tel. 0187-920-367, mobile 349-058-4155, www.ariadimare.info, ask at Billy's if no one's home).

$ Ostello 5-Terre, Manarola's modern and pleasant hostel, occupies the former parochial school above the church square and offers 48 beds in four- to six-bed rooms. Nicola and Riccardo run a calm and peaceful place—it's not a party hostel—and quiet is greatly appreciated. They rent dorm rooms as doubles. Reserve well in advance. Full means full—they don't accommodate the desperate on the floor (Easter-mid-Oct: dorm beds-€24, Db-€65-70, Qb-€100-110; 20 percent less off-season, closed Nov-Feb, not co-ed except for couples and families, no membership necessary, open to all ages, optional €5 breakfast and €6 pasta, office closed 13:00-16:00, rooms closed 10:00-16:00, strict midnight curfew, laundry, safes, phone cards, Internet access, book exchange, elevator, Via B. Riccobaldi 21, tel. 0187-920-215, fax 0187-920-218, www.hostel5terre.com, info@hostel5terre.com).

For Drivers: **$$$ Hotel il Saraceno,** with seven spacious, modern rooms, is a deal for drivers. Located above Manarola in the tiny town of Volastra (chock-full of vacationing Germans and Italians in summer), it's serene, clean, and right by the shuttle bus to Manarola (Db-€100, buffet breakfast, Wi-Fi, free parking, Via Volastra 8, tel. 0187-760-081, fax 0187-760-791, www.thesaraceno .com, hotel@thesaraceno.com, friendly Antonella).

Eating in Manarola

Many hardworking places line the main drag. The Scorza family works hard at **Trattoria il Porticciolo** (free glass of *sciacchetrà* dessert wine with this book, closed Wed, below train tracks at Via R. Birolli 92, tel. 0187-920-083). The harborside **Marina Piccola** is famous for great views, lousy service, and gouging naive tourists.

Trattoria dal Billy, hiding out high on the hill, is a hit, with good food and impressive views over the valley. With Edoardo and Dario's black pasta with seafood and squid ink, green pasta with artichokes, mixed seafood starters, and homemade desserts, many find it worth the climb. Dinner reservations are a must (€11 pastas, €14 *secondi,* generally daily 8:00-10:00 & 12:00-15:00 & 19:00-23:30, sometimes closed Thu, Via Aldo Rollandi 122, tel. 0187-920-628).

Corniglia (Town #3)

This is the quiet town—the only one of the five not on the water—with a mellow main square. According to a (likely fanciful) local

legend, the town was originally settled by a Roman farmer who named it for his mother, Cornelia (how Corniglia is pronounced). The town and its ancient residents produced a wine so famous that—some say—vases found at Pompeii touted its virtues. Regardless of the veracity of the legends, wine remains Corniglia's lifeblood today. Follow the pungent smell of ripe grapes into an alley cellar and get a local to let you dip a straw into a keg. Remote and less visited than the other Cinque Terre towns, Corniglia has fewer tourists, cooler temperatures, a few restaurants, a windy overlook on its promontory, and plenty of private rooms for rent (ask at any bar or shop, no cheaper than other towns). If you think of the Cinque Terre as the Beatles, Corniglia is Ringo.

Orientation to Corniglia

Arrival in Corniglia

From the station, a footpath zigzags up nearly 400 steps to the town. Or take the green shuttle bus, generally timed to meet arriving trains (€1.50 one-way, €2.50 round-trip, free with Cinque Terre Park Card, 2/hour). Before leaving for the bus, confirm departure times on the schedule posted at the stop. If you're driving, be aware that only residents can park on the main road between the recommended Villa Cecio and the point where the steep switchback staircase meets the road. Beyond that area, parking is €1.50 per hour.

Corniglia

To Vernazza

200 Meters
200 Yards

HUNDREDS OF STEPS

"CIAPPÀ" SQUARE & BUS STOP

Harbor

SANTA MARIA BELVEDERE

LARGO TARAGIO, ORATORY & ❹

Ligurian Sea

To Manarola

TRAIN STATION

SWIMMING

❶ Pan e Vin Bar (Ricci Rooms Check-In)
❷ Villa Cecio Rooms
❸ Corniglia Hostel
❹ La Lanterna Restaurant
❺ Osteria Mananan
❻ Enoteca il Pirun
❼ La Posada Ristorante
❽ Gelateria
❾ Butiega Shop

Self-Guided Walk

Welcome to Corniglia

We'll explore this tiny town—population 240—and end at a scenic viewpoint.

• *Begin near the bus stop, located at a...*

Town Square: The gateway to this community is "Ciappà" square, with an ATM, phone booth, old wine press, and bus stop. The Cinque Terre's designation as a national park sparked a revitalization of the town. Corniglia's young generation is more likely now to stay put, rather than migrate into big cities the way locals did in the past.

• *Stroll the spine of Corniglia, Via Fieschi. In the fall, the smell of grapes (on their way to becoming wine) wafts from busy cellars. Along this main street, you'll see...*

Corniglia's Enticing Shops: Alberto's Gelateria dishes up the best homemade gelato in town. Before ordering, get a free taste of Alberto's *miele di Corniglia*, made from local honey. His local lemon slush takes pucker to new heights. **Enoteca il Pirun**—named for a type of oddly shaped old-fashioned wine pitcher designed to aerate the wine and give the alcohol more kick—is located in a cool cantina at Via Fieschi 115. Sample some local wines (generally free for small tastes). If you buy something, they may gift you with a souvenir bib. In the **Butiega**

shop at Via Fieschi 142, Vincenzo and Diego sell organic local specialties (daily 8:00-19:30). For picnickers, they offer €2.50 made-to-order ham-and-cheese sandwiches and a fun €3.50 *antipasto misto* to go. (There are good places to picnic farther along on this walk.)

• *Following Via Fieschi, you'll end up at the...*

Main Square: On Largo Taragio, tables from two bars and a trattoria spill around a WWI memorial and the town's old well. It once piped in natural spring water from the hillside to locals living without plumbing. What looks like a church is the Oratory of Santa Caterina. (An oratory is a kind of a spiritual clubhouse for a service group doing social work in the name of the Catholic Church.) Behind the oratory, you'll find a clearing that local children have made into a soccer field. The stone benches and viewpoint make this a peaceful place for a picnic (less crowded than the end-of-town viewpoint, described below).

• *Opposite the oratory, notice how steps lead steeply down on Via alla Marina to Corniglia's non-beach. It's a five-minute paved climb to sunning rocks, a shower, and a small deck (with a treacherous entry into the water). From the square, continue up Via Fieschi to the...*

End-of-Town Viewpoint: The Santa Maria Belvedere, named for a church that once stood here, marks the scenic end of Corniglia. This is a super picnic spot. From here, look high to the west, where the village and sanctuary of San Bernardino straddle a ridge (a good starting point for a hike; accessible by shuttle bus from Monterosso or a long uphill hike from Vernazza). Below is the tortuous harbor, where locals hoist their boats onto the cruel rocks.

Sights in Corniglia

Beaches—This hilltop town has rocky sea access below its train station (toward Manarola). Once a beach, it's all been washed away and offers no services. Look for signs that say *al mare* or *Marina*. A trail leads from the town center steeply down to sunning rocks on the closest thing Corniglia has to a beach (with a shower).

The infamous **Guvano beach** (a bit along the coast toward Vernazza) is now essentially closed down. Guvano was created by an 1893 landslide that cost the village a third of its farmland. Notorious throughout Italy as a nude beach, Guvano was accessed via an unused train tunnel and attracted visitors with an appetite for drug use. Now the tunnel is closed, and the national park wants people to keep their clothes on and forget about Guvano.

THE CINQUE TERRE

Sleeping in Corniglia

(€1 = about $1.40, country code: 39)

Perched high above the sea on a hilltop, Corniglia has plenty of private rooms. To get to the town from the station, catch the shuttle bus or make the 15-minute uphill hike. The town is riddled with humble places that charge too much (generally Db-€65) and have meager business skills and a limited ability to converse with tourists—so it's almost never full.

$$ Cristiana Ricci is an exception to the rule. She communicates well and is reliable, renting four small, clean, and peaceful rooms—two with kitchens and one with a terrace and sweeping view—just inland from the bus stop (Db-€60-70, Qb-€90, €10/day less when you stay 2 or more nights, free Internet access, check in at the Pan e Vin bar at Via Fieschi 123, mobile 338-937-6547, cri_affittacamere@virgilio.it, Stefano). Her mom rents a big, modern apartment (€90 for 2-4 people).

$$ Villa Cecio (pronounced "chay-choe") feels like an abandoned hotel. They offer eight well-worn rooms on the outskirts of town, with saggy beds and little character or warmth (Db-€65 promised in 2012, breakfast-€5, cash preferred, great views, on main road 200 yards toward Vernazza at Via Serra 58, tel. 0187-812-043, fax 0187-812-138, mobile 334-350-6637, www.cecio5terre.com, info@cecio5terre.com, Giacinto). They also rent eight similar rooms (Db-€60) in an annex on the square where the bus stops.

$ Corniglia Hostel was formerly the town's schoolhouse. It rents 24 beds in a pastel-yellow building up some steps from the main square where the bus stops. The playground in front is often busy with happy kids. Despite its institutional atmosphere, the hostel's prices, central location, and bright and clean rooms ensure its popularity. Its hotelesque double rooms are open to anyone (€24/bed in two 8-bed dorms, €27 with minimal breakfast; four Db-€55, €60 with breakfast; air-con, lockers, Internet access, Wi-Fi, self-serve laundry, mountain bikes for rent, no public spaces except lobby, office open 7:00-13:00 & 15:00-24:00, rooms closed 13:00-15:00, 1:30 curfew, Via alla Stazione 3, tel. 0187-812-559, fax 0187-763-984, www.ostellocorniglia.com but reserve at www.hostelworld.com, ostellocorniglia@gmail.com, helpful Andrea).

Eating in Corniglia

Corniglia has few restaurants.

The trattoria **La Lanterna,** on the main square, is the most atmospheric (but without particularly charming service).

Osteria Mananan—between the Ciappà bus stop and the main square on Via Fieschi—serves what many consider the best food in town in its small, stony, elegant interior (Fri-Wed 12:15-14:30 & 19:45-21:15, closed Tue, no outdoor seating, tel. 0187-821-166).

Enoteca il Pirun, also on Via Fieschi, has a small restaurant above the wine bar, where Mario serves typical local dishes (€28 fixed-price meal includes homemade wine, daily 12:00-16:00 & 19:30-23:30, tel. 0187-812-315).

La Posada Ristorante offers dinner in a garden under trees, overlooking the Ligurian Sea. To get here, stroll out of town to the top of the stairs from the station (€10 pastas, €10 *secondi*, €15 tourist *menu*, nightly from 19:00, tel. 0187-821-174).

Vernazza (Town #4)

With the closest thing to a natural harbor—overseen by a ruined castle and a stout stone church—Vernazza is the jewel of the

Cinque Terre. Only the occasional noisy slurping up of the train by the mountain reminds you of the modern world.

The action is at the harbor, where you'll find outdoor restaurants, a bar hanging on the edge of the castle, and a breakwater with a promenade, corralled by a natural amphitheater of terraced hills. In the summer, the beach becomes a soccer field, where teams fielded by local bars and restaurants provide late-night entertainment. In the dark, locals fish off the promontory, using glowing bobbers that shine in the waves.

Proud of their Vernazzan heritage, the town's 500 residents like to brag: "Vernazza is locally owned. Portofino has sold out." Fearing the change it would bring, keep-Vernazza-small proponents stopped the construction of a major road into the town and region. Families are tight and go back centuries; several generations stay together. In the winter, the population shrinks, as many people return to their more comfortable big-city apartments to spend the money they reaped during the tourist season.

Leisure time is devoted to taking part in the *passeggiata*—strolling lazily together up and down the main street. Sit on a bench and study the passersby doing their *vasche* (laps). Explore the characteristic alleys, called *carugi*. Learn—and live—the phrase *"la vita pigra di Vernazza"* (the lazy life of Vernazza).

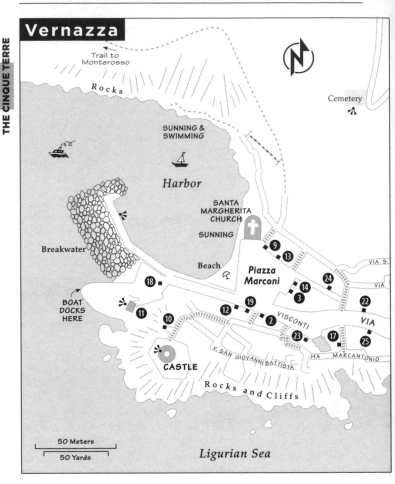

Orientation to Vernazza

Tourist Information

The TI/park information/train ticket office is one desk buried in a gift shop between the two tracks at the train station (daily 8:00-19:30, tel. 0187-812-524). Some of the staff may ring the owner of the room you have reserved as a courtesy, but they cannot make reservations. Public WCs are nearby in the station.

Arrival in Vernazza

By Train: Vernazza's train station is only about three cars long, but the trains are much longer, so most of the cars come to a stop in a long, dark tunnel. Get out anyway, and walk through the tunnel to the station.

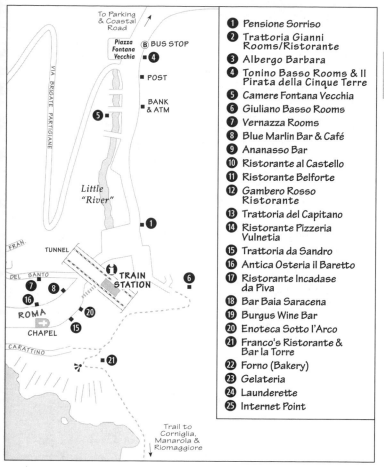

To Parking & Coastal Road

Piazza Fontana Vecchia

Ⓑ BUS STOP

POST

BANK & ATM

VIA BRIGATE PARTIGIANE

Little "River"

FRAN.

TUNNEL

DEL SANTO

ROMA

CHAPEL

CARATTINO

Trail to Corniglia, Manarola & Riomaggiore

TRAIN STATION

❶ Pensione Sorriso
❷ Trattoria Gianni Rooms/Ristorante
❸ Albergo Barbara
❹ Tonino Basso Rooms & Il Pirata della Cinque Terre
❺ Camere Fontana Vecchia
❻ Giuliano Basso Rooms
❼ Vernazza Rooms
❽ Blue Marlin Bar & Café
❾ Ananasso Bar
❿ Ristorante al Castello
⓫ Ristorante Belforte
⓬ Gambero Rosso Ristorante
⓭ Trattoria del Capitano
⓮ Ristorante Pizzeria Vulnetia
⓯ Trattoria da Sandro
⓰ Antica Osteria il Baretto
⓱ Ristorante Incadase da Piva
⓲ Bar Baia Saracena
⓳ Burgus Wine Bar
⓴ Enoteca Sotto l'Arco
㉑ Franco's Ristorante & Bar la Torre
㉒ Forno (Bakery)
㉓ Gelateria
㉔ Launderette
㉕ Internet Point

By Car: There's a nonresident parking lot, but be aware that parking can be tough from May through September (€2/hour, €12/24 hours, cash only, about 500 yards above town, pay first at the parking stand before getting your spot). A hardworking shuttle service, generally with friendly English-speaking Beppe, Simone, or Pietro behind the wheel, connects the lot to the top of town (€1.50, free with Cinque Terre Park Card, 3-4/hour, runs 7:00-19:00). Yellow lines mark parking spots for residents. The highest lot (a side-trip uphill) is for overnight stays.

Helpful Hints

Internet Access: The **Blue Marlin Bar,** run by Massimo and Carmen, has the lowest prices and longest hours (€0.10/minute, Internet available Thu-Tue 10:00-22:30—but opens earlier for breakfast, closed Wed). The slick, six-terminal **Internet Point,** run by Alberto and Isabella, is in the village center (€0.15/minute, €0.10/minute after 30 minutes, daily June-Oct 9:30-23:00, until 20:00 Nov-May, Wi-Fi, will burn your digital photos to a CD or DVD for €5). The recommended **Il Pirata delle Cinque Terre** bar, at the top of the town, offers free Wi-Fi.

Laundry: Lavanderia il Carugetto is completely self-serve and hides out on a narrow lane a block off the main drag (coin-op, €6/wash, €5/dry, daily 8:00-22:00, opposite the pharmacy—go ten steps up and turn left, operated by Domenico and Barbara at the fish shop).

Massage: Stephanie, an American expat, gives a good, strong therapeutic massage in a neat little studio at the top of town. Famous among locals as the physical therapist who massaged an old woman back to health, Stephanie can counsel you on tuning up your body while giving insights into the social intricacies of the village (€50/hour, mobile 338-9429-494, stephsette@gmail.com). **Kate** offers a softer and more aromatic style: reflexology, holistic, and hot stone massage (mobile 333-568-4653, www.vernazzamassage5terre.com).

Best Views: A steep 10-minute hike in either direction from Vernazza gives you a classic village photo op (for the best light, head toward Corniglia in the morning, and toward Monterosso in the evening).

Self-Guided Walks

Welcome to Vernazza

This tour includes Vernazza's characteristic town squares and ends on its scenic breakwater.

• *From the train station, walk uphill until you hit the parking lot, with a bank, a post office, and a barrier that keeps out all but service vehicles. Vernazza's shuttle buses run from here to the parking lot and into the hills. Walk to the tidy, modern square called...*

Fontana Vecchia: Named after a long-gone fountain, this is where older locals remember the river filled with townswomen doing their washing. Now they enjoy checking on the baby ducks. A lane leads from here up to the cemetery. Imagine the entire village sadly trudging up here during funerals. (The cemetery is peaceful and evocative at sunset, when the fading light touches each crypt.)

• *Glad to be here in happier times, begin your saunter downhill to the harbor. Just before the* Pensione Sorriso *sign, on your right (big brown wood doors), you'll see the...*

Ambulance Barn: A group of volunteers is always on call for a dash to the hospital, 40 minutes away in La Spezia. Opposite the barn is a big empty lot. Like many landowners, the owner of Pensione Sorriso had plans to expand, but since the 1980s, the government has said "No." While some landowners are frustrated, the old character of these towns survives. A few steps farther down is the town clinic. The *guarda medica* (emergency doctor—see buzzer) sleeps upstairs.

• At the corner across from the playground, you'll see a...

World Wars Monument: Look for a marble plaque in the wall to your left, dedicated to those killed in the World Wars. Not a family in Vernazza was spared. Listed on the left are soldiers *morti in combattimento,* who died in World War I; on the right is the World War II section. Some were deported to *Germania;* others—labeled *Part* (stands for *partigiani,* or partisans, generally communists)—were killed while fighting against Mussolini. Cynics considered partisans less than heroes. After 1943, Hitler called up Italian boys over 15. Rather than die on the front for Hitler, they escaped to the hills. They became "resistance fighters" in order to remain free.

The path to Corniglia leaves from here (behind and above the plaque). Behind you is a small square and playground, decorated with three millstones, once used to grind local olives into oil. There's a good chance you'll see an expat mom here at the village playground with her kids. I've met many American women who fell in love with a local guy, stayed, and are now happily raising families here. (But I've rarely met an American guy who moved in with a local girl.)

From here, Vernazza's tiny river goes underground. Until the 1950s, the river ran openly through the center of town. Old-timers recall the days before the breakwater, when the river cascaded down and the surf sent waves rolling up Vernazza's main drag. Back then, this place was nicknamed "Little Venice" for the series of romantic bridges that arched over the stream, connecting the two sides of the town before the main road was built.

Before the tracks (on the left), the wall has 10 spaces, one reserved for each political party's ads during elections—a kind of campaign pollution control. On the wall under the tracks (right side), a big photo shows the old road into town before there were cars, back when vineyards entirely covered the hills. A map shows the region's hiking trails—trail #2 is the basic favorite. The green box on the wall (on the right) lists which days volunteer ambulance drivers are on call. You'll notice that family names repeat a lot. A few big families dominate the town, and in the local dialect, everyone in your village is called "cousin." Finally, a community event board says what's happening in town. The second set of tracks (nearer the harbor) was recently renovated to lessen the disruptive noise, but locals say it made no difference.

• *Follow the road downhill to...*

Vernazza's "Business Center": Here, you'll pass many locals doing their *vasche* (laps). At Enoteca Sotto l'Arco, Gerry and Paola sell wine—they can uncork it and throw in plastic glasses—and delightful jars of local pesto, which goes great on bread (Via Roma 70). Next, you'll pass the Blue Marlin Bar (Vernazza's top night-spot) and the tiny Chapel of Santa Marta (the small stone chapel with iron grillwork over the window), where Mass is celebrated only on special Sundays. Farther down, you'll walk by a grocery, *gelateria*, bakery, pharmacy, another grocery, and another *gelateria*. There are plenty of fun and cheap food-to-go options here.

• *On the left, in front of the second* gelateria, *an arch (with a peaceful little sitting perch atop it) leads to what was a beach, where the town's stream used to hit the sea back in the 1970s. Continue down to the...*

Harbor Square and Breakwater: Vernazza, with the only natural harbor of the Cinque Terre, was established as the sole place boats could pick up the fine local wine. The two-foot-high square stone at the foot of the stairs by the Burgus Wine Bar is marked *Sasso del Sego* (stone of tallow). Workers crushed animal flesh and fat in its basin to make tallow, which drained out of the tiny hole below. The tallow was then used to waterproof boats or wine barrels. For more town history, step into the Burgus to see fascinating old photos of Vernazza on the wall. Stonework is the soul of the region. Take some time to appreciate the impressive stonework of the restaurant interiors facing the harbor.

On the far side (behind Ristorante Pizzeria Vulnetia), peek into the tiny street with its commotion of arches. Vernazza's most characteristic side streets, called *carugi*, lead up from here. The trail (above the church, toward Monterosso) leads to the quintessential view of Vernazza.

Located in front of the harborside church, the tiny piazza—decorated with a river-rock mosaic—is a popular hangout spot. It's where Vernazza's old ladies soak up the last bit of sun, and kids enjoy a patch of level ball field.

Vernazza's harborfront church is unusual for its strange entry-way, which faces east (altar side). With relative peace and pros-perity in the 16th century, the townspeople doubled the church in size, causing it to overtake a little piazza that once faced the west facade. From the square, use the "new" entry and climb the steps, keeping an eye out for the level necessary to keep the church high and dry. Inside, the lighter pillars in the back mark the 16th-century extension. Three historic portable crosses hanging on the walls are carried through town during Easter processions. They are replicas of crosses that Vernazza ships once carried on crusades to the Holy Land.

• *Finish your town tour seated out on the breakwater (perhaps with a glass of local white wine or something more interesting from a nearby bar—borrow the glass, they don't mind). Face the town, and see...*

The Harbor: In a moderate storm, you'd be soaked, as waves routinely crash over the *molo* (breakwater, built in 1972). Waves can even wash away tourists squinting excitedly into their cameras. (I've seen it happen.) In 2007, an American woman was swept away and killed by a rogue wave. Enjoy the new waterfront piazza—carefully.

The train line (to your left) was constructed in 1874 to tie together a newly united Italy, and linked Turin and Genoa with Rome. A second line (hidden in a tunnel at this point) was built in the 1920s. The yellow building alongside the tracks was Vernazza's first train station. You can see the four bricked-up alcoves where people once waited for trains. Notice the wonderful new concrete sunbathing strip (and place for late-night privacy) laid below the tracks along the rocks.

Vernazza's fishing fleet is down to just a couple of boats (with the net spools). Vernazzans are still more likely to own a boat than a car, and it's said that you stand a better chance of surviving if you mess with a local man's wife than with his boat. Boats are on buoys, except in winter or when the red storm flag (see pole at start of breakwater) indicates bad seas. At these times, the boats are pulled up onto the square—which is usually reserved for restaurant tables. In the 1970s, tiny Vernazza had one of Italy's top water polo teams, and the harbor was their "pool." Later, when the league required a real pool, Vernazza dropped out.

The Castle: On the far right, the castle, which is now a grassy park with great views (and nothing but stones), still guards the

town (€1.50 donation supports the local emergency doctor and volunteer ambulance group, daily 10:00-19:00; from harbor, take stairs by Trattoria Gianni and follow *Ristorante al Castello* signs, tower is a few steps beyond). This was the town's watchtower back in pirate days, and a Nazi lookout in World War II. The castle tower looks new because it was rebuilt after the British bombed it, chasing out the Germans. The highest umbrellas mark the recommended Ristorante Al Castello. The squat tower on the water is great for a glass of wine or a meal. From the breakwater, you could follow the rope to the Ristorante Belforte and pop inside, past the actual submarine door. A photo of a major storm showing the entire tower under a wave (not uncommon in the winter) hangs near the bar.

The Town: Vernazza has two halves. *Sciuiu* (Vernazzan dialect for "flowery") is the sunny side on the left, and *luvegu* (dank) is the shady side on the right. Houses below the castle were connected by an interior arcade—ideal for fleeing attacks. The "Ligurian pastel" colors are regulated by a commissioner of good taste in the regional government. The square before you is locally famous for some of the area's finest restaurants. The big red central house—on the site where Genoan warships were built in the 12th century—used to be a guardhouse.

In the Middle Ages, there was no beach or square. The water went right up to the buildings, where boats would tie up, Venetian-style. Imagine what Vernazza looked like in those days, when it was the biggest and richest of the Cinque Terre towns. Buildings had a water gate (facing today's square) and a front door on the higher inland side. There was no pastel plaster, just fine stonework (traces of which survive above the Trattoria del Capitano). Apart from the added plaster, the general shape and size of the town has changed little in five centuries. Survey the windows and notice inhabitants quietly gazing back.

Above the Town: The small, round tower above the red guardhouse—another part of the city fortifications—reminds us of Vernazza's importance in the Middle Ages, when it was a key ally of Genoa (whose archenemies were the other maritime republics, especially Pisa). Franco's Ristorante and Bar la Torre, just behind the tower, welcomes hikers who are finishing, starting, or simply contemplating the Corniglia-Vernazza hike, with great town views. That tower recalls a time when the entire town was fortified by a stone wall. Vineyards fill the mountainside beyond the town. Notice the many terraces. Someone—probably after too much of that local wine—calculated that the roughly 3,000 miles of dry-stone walls built to terrace the region's vineyards have the same amount of stonework as the Great Wall of China.

Wine production is down nowadays, as the younger residents choose less physical work. But locals still maintain their tiny plots and proudly serve their family wines. The patchwork of local vineyards is atomized and complex because of inheritance traditions. Historically, families divided their land between their children. Parents wanted each child to get some good land. Because some lots were "kissed by the sun" while others were shady, the lots were split into increasingly tiny and eventually unviable pieces.

A single steel train line winds up the gully behind the tower. It is for the vintner's *trenino,* the tiny service train. Play "Where's *trenino?*" and see if you can find two trains. The vineyards once stretched as high as you can see, but since fewer people sweat in the fields these days, the most distant terraces have gone wild again.

The Church, School, and City Hall: Vernazza's Ligurian Gothic church, built with black stones quarried from Punta Mesco (the distant point behind you), dates from 1318. Note the gray stone that marks the church's 16th-century expansion. The gray-and-red house above the spire is the local elementary school (about 25 children attend; education through age 14 is obligatory). High-schoolers go to the "big city": La Spezia. The red building to the right of the schoolhouse, a former monastery, is the City Hall. Vernazza and Corniglia function as one community. Through most of the 1990s, the local government was Communist. In 1999, residents elected a coalition of many parties working to rise above ideologies and simply make Vernazza a better place. That practical notion of government continues here today. Finally, on the top of the hill, with the best view of all, is the town cemetery.

Sights in Vernazza

Tuesday-Morning Market—Vernazza's skimpy business community is augmented Tuesday mornings (8:00-13:00) when a meager gang of cars and trucks pulls into town for a tailgate market.

Beach—The harbor's sandy cove has sunning rocks and showers by the breakwater. There's also a ladder on the breakwater for deep-water access. The new sunbathing lane directly under the church also has a shower.

Boat Rental—Vincenzo of Nord Est rents canoes and small motorboats from his stand on the harbor, and also takes people out for mini-cruises. With a rental boat, you can reach a tiny *acqua pendente* (waterfall) cove between Vernazza and Monterosso; locals call it their *laguna blu* (motorboats-€60/2 hours, €80/4 hours, plus gas—usually about €15, includes snorkeling gear, May-Oct only, mobile 338-700-0436, info@manuela-vernazza.com).

Shuttle Bus Joyride—For a cheap and scenic joyride, with a chance to chat about the region with friendly Beppe, Simone, or Pietro, ride the shuttle bus from the top of town for the entire route for the cost of a round-trip ticket. Some buses also head to two sanctuaries in the hills above town (5/day—usually at 7:00, 9:45, 12:00, 15:00, and 17:30; schedule posted at park office, train station, and bus stop in front of post office; €2.50 one-way, free with Cinque Terre Park Card, churches at sanctuaries usually closed). The high-country 40-minute loop—buses are marked *Drignana*—gives you lots of scenery without having to hike (don't take buses marked *No panoramic*, as these won't take scenic routes).

Nightlife in Vernazza

Vernazza's younger generation of restaurant workers lets loose after-hours. They work hard through the tourist season, travel in the winter, speak English, and enjoy connecting with international visitors. After the restaurants close down, the town is quiet except for a couple of nightspots. For more information on the Blue Marlin, Ananasso, Il Pirata, and Ristorante Incadase, see their listings under "Eating in Vernazza," later. All bars must close by 24:00.

Blue Marlin Bar dominates the late-night scene with a mix of locals and tourists, home-cooked food until 22:00, good drinks, and piano jam sessions. If you're young and hip, this is *the* place to hang out. If you play the piano, you're welcome to contribute to the scene.

Ananasso Bar offers early-evening happy-hour fun and cocktails (called *"aperitivi"*) that both locals and visitors enjoy. Its harborfront tables get the last sunshine of the day.

Burgus Wine Bar, chic and cool with a jazzy ambience, is a popular early-evening and after-dinner harborside hangout. Sip local wine or a cocktail. Valerio and Lorenza specialize in Ligurian wines and can explain the historic town photos and museum cases of artifacts (closed Tue, free Wi-Fi with a drink, Piazza Marconi 4).

Il Pirata delle Cinque Terre, at the top of the town, features the entertaining Cannoli brothers, who fill a happy crowd of tourists with wonderful Sicilian pastries and drinks each evening. Many come for dinner and end up staying because of these two wild and crazy guys and the camaraderie they create among their diners (erratic hours driven by demand, free Wi-Fi).

Ristorante Incadase da Piva (tucked up the lane behind the pharmacy) is the haunt of Piva, Vernazza's troubadour. Piva often gets out his guitar and sings traditional local songs as well as his own compositions. If you're looking for a local Hemingway, check here.

Top of the Town: A couple of bars with light meals have great perches high above the town (on the trail to Corniglia).

Really Late: There's a little cave on the beach just under the church that lends itself to fun in the wee hours, when everything else is closed.

Sleeping in Vernazza

(€1 = about $1.40, country code: 39)
Vernazza, the spindly and salty essence of the Cinque Terre, is my top choice for a home base. Off-season (Oct-March), you

can generally arrive without a reservation and find a place, but at other times, it's smart to book ahead (especially June-July and weekends).

People recommended here are listed for their communication skills (they speak English, have email, and are reliable with bookings) and because they rent several rooms. Consequently, my recommendations cost more than comparable rooms you'll find if you shop around. Comparison-shopping will likely save you €10-20 per double per night—and often get you a better place and view to boot. The real Vernazza gems are stray single rooms with owners who have no interest in booking in advance or messing with email. Arrive by early afternoon and drop by any shop or bar and ask; most locals know someone who rents rooms.

Anywhere you stay here requires some climbing, but keep in mind that more climbing means better views. Most do not include breakfast (for suggestions, see "Eating in Vernazza," later). Cash is preferred or required almost everywhere. Night noise can be a problem if you're near the station. Rooms on the harbor come with church bells (but only between 7:00 and 22:00).

Pensions

These pensions are located on the Vernazza map, earlier in this chapter.

$$$ Pensione Sorriso, the oldest pension in town (where I stayed on my first visit in 1975), rents 19 overpriced rooms above the train station. While the main building has the charm, it comes with train noise and saggy beds; the annex, up the street, is in a quieter apartment that feels forgotten (S-€65, Sb-€80, D-€100, Db-€140-150, Tb-€130, includes breakfast, some with air-con, Wi-Fi, Via Gavino 4, tel. 0187-812-224, fax 0187-821-198, www.pensionesorriso.com, info@pensionesorriso.com, Francesca and Aldo).

$$$ Trattoria Gianni rents 27 small rooms and three apartments just under the castle. The rooms are in three buildings—one funky, two modern—up a hundred tight, winding spiral stairs. The funky ones, which may or may not have private baths, are artfully decorated à la shipwreck, with tiny balconies and grand sea views *(con vista sul mare)*. The comfy new *(nuovo)* rooms lack views. Both have modern bathrooms and access to a super-scenic cliff-hanging guests' garden. Steely Marisa requires check-in before 16:00

or a phone call to explain when you're coming. Emanuele (Gianni's son, who now runs the restaurant), Simona, and the staff speak a little English (S-€45, D-€80, Db-€100-120, Tb-€120-140, 10 percent discount with cash and this book—request when you reserve, cancellations less than a week in advance are charged one night's deposit, closed Jan-Feb, Piazza Marconi 5, tel. & fax 0187-812-228, tel. 0187-821-003, on Wed call mobile 393-9008-155 instead, www.giannifranzi.it, info@giannifranzi.it). Pick up your keys at Trattoria Gianni's restaurant on the harbor square.

$$ Albergo Barbara rents nine simple, clean, and modern rooms overlooking the harbor square—most with small windows and small views. It's run by English-speaking Giuseppe and his no-nonsense Swiss wife, Patricia (D-€55, Db-€65-70, big Db with nice harbor view-€110, extra bed-€10, 2-night stay preferred, closed Dec-Feb, reserve online with credit card but pay cash, free Wi-Fi, Piazza Marconi 30, tel. & fax 0187-812-398, mobile 338-793-3261, www.albergobarbara.it, info@albergobarbara.it).

Private Rooms (Affitta Camere)

Vernazza is honeycombed with private rooms year-round, offering the best values in town. Owners may be reluctant to reserve rooms far in advance. It's easiest to call a day or two ahead or simply show up in the morning and look around. Doubles cost €55-100, depending on the view, season, and plumbing—you get what you pay for. Most places accept only cash. Some have killer views, come with lots of stairs, and cost the same as a small, dark place on a back lane over the train tracks. Little English is spoken at many of these places. If you call to let them know your arrival time (or call when you arrive, using your mobile phone or the pay phone just below the station), they'll meet you at the train station.

Well-Managed and Well-Appointed Rooms in the Inland Part of Town

$$$ Tonino Basso rents four sparkling-clean, modern rooms—at a steep price. Each room has its own computer for free Internet access. He's in the only building in Vernazza with an elevator. You get tranquility and air-conditioning, but no views (Sb-€65, Db-€120, Tb-€150, Qb-€180, prices go down Nov-March, call Tonino's mobile number upon arrival and he'll meet you, tel. 0187-821-264, mobile 335-269-436, fax 0187-812-807, toninobasso @libero.it). If you can't locate Tonino, ask his friends at Enoteca Sotto l'Arco at Via Roma 70.

$$ Camere Fontana Vecchia is a delightful place, with four bright, spacious, quiet rooms and an apartment near the post office (no view). As the only place in Vernazza with almost no stairs to climb and the sound of a babbling brook outside your window, it's one of the best values in town (D-€70, Db-€80, T-€95, Tb-€110, super-trendy 2-person apartment-€100, fans and heat, open all year, Via Gavino 15, tel. 0187-821-130, mobile 333-454-9371, fax 0187-812-261, m.annamaria@libero.it, youthful and efficient Anna speaks English). If no one answers, ask at Enoteca Sotto l'Arco on the main drag.

$$ **Giuliano Basso** rents four pleasant rooms, crafted with care, just above town in the terraced wilds (sea views from terraces). Straddling a ravine among orange trees, it's an artfully decorated Robinson Crusoe-chic wonderland, proudly built out of stone by Giuliano himself—the town's last stone-layer, who "has stone in his blood" (Db-€80, Db suite with air-con-€100, Db suite with private rooftop balcony-€100, extra bed-€25, fridge access, free Internet access, more train noise than others, above train station, take the ramp just before Pensione Sorriso, mobile 333-341-4792, or have Enoteca Sotto l'Arco contact him, www.cdh.it/giuliano, giuliano@cdh.it).

Other Reliable Places Scattered Through Town and the Harborside

These places are not located on this book's map; ask for directions when you reserve.

$$$ **La Malà** is Vernazza's jetsetter pad. Four pristine white rooms boast four-star-hotel-type extras and a common terrace looking out over the rocky shore (Db-€155, Db suite-€220, includes breakfast at a bar, air-con, Wi-Fi, tel. 334-287-5718, fax 0187-812-218, www.lamala.it, info@lamala.it, Giamba and Armanda). It's a climb—way, way up to the top of town—but they'll gladly carry your bags to and from the station. They also rent the simpler "Armanda's Room" nearby (no view, Db-€75, ring bell at Piazza Marconi 15).

$$$ **Martina Callo**'s four air-conditioned rooms overlook the square; they're up plenty of steps near the silent-at-night church tower (room #1: Tb-€110 or Qb-€120 with harbor view; room #2: huge Qb family room with no view-€110; room #3: Db with grand view terrace-€100; room #4: roomy Db with no view-€60; free Wi-Fi, ring bell at Piazza Marconi 26, tel. & fax 0187-812-365, mobile 329-435-5344, www.roomartina.com, roomartina @roomartina.com).

$$ **Monica Lercari** rents several classy rooms with modern comforts, perched at the top of town. Guests are welcome to borrow the family rowboat or mountain bike (Db-€80, seaview D-€100, grand sea-view terrace D-€120, "honeymoon suite" Db-€180, includes breakfast, air-con, Wi-Fi, next to recommended Ristorante al Castello, tel. 0187-812-296, alcastello vernazza@yahoo.it).

$$ Memo Rooms has three clean and spacious rooms that offer good value. They overlook the main street, in what feels like a miniature hotel. Enrica will meet you if you call upon arrival (Db-€70, Via Roma 15, tel. 0187-812-360, mobile 338-285-2385, www.memorooms.com, info@memorooms.com).

$$ Nicolina rents five recently renovated units with double-paned windows. Two rooms are in the center over the pharmacy, up a few steep steps—one has only sleeper sofas (Db-€80); two others are in a different building beyond the church with great views (Db-€100, Tb-€120, Qb-€150); and the last unit is a two-bedroom quadruple with even better views (€200). Inquire at Pizzeria Vulnetia on the harbor square (Piazza Marconi 29, tel. & fax 0187-821-193, www.camerenicolina.it, camerenicolina.info@cdh.it).

$$ Rosa Vitali rents two four-person apartments across from the pharmacy overlooking the main street (and beyond the train noise). One has a terrace and fridge (top floor); the other has windows and a full kitchen (Db-€95, Tb-€115, Qb-€125, reception at Via Visconti 10 between the grotto and Piazza Marconi, tel. 0187-821-181, mobile 340-267-5009, www.rosacamere.it, rosa.vitali@libero.it).

$$ Francamaria and her kind husband Andrea rent eight sharp, comfortable, and creatively renovated but expensive rooms— all described in detail on her website. While their reception desk is on the harbor square (on the ground floor facing the harbor at Piazza Marconi 30—don't confuse it with Albergo Barbara at same address), the rooms they manage are all over town (Db-€80-120 depending on size and view, Qb-€125-160, extra person-€20, tel. & fax 0187-812-002, mobile 328-711-9728, www.francamaria.com, francamaria@francamaria.com).

More Private Rooms in Vernazza

$$ Maria Capellini rents a couple of simple, clean rooms, including one on the ground floor right on the harbor (Db with kitchen-€85, Tb-€110, cash only, fans, mobile 338-436-3411, www.mariacapellini.com, mariacapellini@hotmail.it, Maria and Giacomo).

$$ Il Pirata delle Cinque Terre rents two basic rooms with the sounds of the river below. Managed by Noelia and Leyla, wives of the Cannoli brothers (see listing under "Eating in Vernazza"), the rooms are at the top of the town, 100 yards beyond their bar (Db-€90, Tb-€130, Qb-€160, includes breakfast with this book at Il Pirata bar—which also functions as the reception, 2-night minimum, cash only, tel. 0187-812-047, mobile 338-596-2503, www.ilpiratarooms.com, ilpiratarooms@libero.it).

$$ Ivo's Camere rents two simple no-terrace rooms high above the main street, as well as a studio apartment (Db-€75, studio-€100, free Wi-Fi, Via Roma 6, reception at Pizzeria Fratelli Basso—Via Roma 1, tel. 0187-821-042, mobile 333-477-5521, www .ivocamere.com, post@ivocamere.com).

$$ Vernazza Rooms, run by Daria Bianchi, Chiara, and Davide, rents 12 decent rooms from their office near the station. Four rooms are above the Blue Marlin Bar looking down on the main street, and eight are below the City Hall (Db-€60-95, Qb-€100-120, fans, reception next to Blue Marlin Bar at Via del Santo 9, tel. 0187-812-151, mobile 338-581-4688 or 338-418-8696, www.vernazzarooms.com, info@vernazzarooms.com).

$$ Emanuela Colombo has two rooms—one spacious and basic on the harbor square, the other *molto* chic and located on a quiet side street (Db-€90, Tb-€110, tel. 339-834-2486, www .vacanzemanuela.it, manucap64@libero.it).

More Options: **$$ Affitta Camere Alberto Basso** (a clean, modern room with a noisy harbor/piazza view, Db-€75, check in at Internet Point, albertobasso@hotmail.com); **$$ Capitano Rooms** (3 recently remodeled rooms above the main drag, Db-€90, ask for Paolo or Barbara at the Trattoria del Capitano restaurant, tel. 0187-812-201); **$$ Eva's Rooms** (3 rooms overlooking main street with train noise, Db-€60-80, ring at Via Roma 56, tel. 0187-821-134, www.evasrooms.it, massimoeva@libero.it); **$$ Manuela Moggia** (3 rooms, Db-€80, Tb-€95, Qb with kitchen-€125, top of the town at Via Gavino 22, tel. 0187-812-397, mobile 333-413-6374, www.manuela-vernazza.com, info@manuela-vernazza.com); and **$$ Elisabetta Rooms** (3 tired rooms at the tip-top of town with Vernazza's ultimate 360-degree roof terrace, Db-€65, Tb-€90, Qb-€100, fans, Via Carattino 62, mobile 347-451-1834, www.elisa bettacarro.it, carroelisabetta@hotmail.com, Elisabetta and Pino).

Eating in Vernazza

Breakfast

Locals take breakfast about as seriously as flossing. A cappuccino and a pastry or a piece of focaccia from a bar or bakery does it. Most of my recommended accommodations don't come with breakfast (when they do, I've noted so in my listings). Assuming you're on your own, you have four basic options: Blue Marlin Bar for its extensive menu, including bacon and eggs; Il Pirata delle Cinque Terre for sugary stuff and a lively welcome; Ananasso Bar for coffee and a sweet roll on the harborfront; or any bakery for picnic goodies.

Blue Marlin Bar (mid-town, just below the train station) serves a good array of clearly priced à la carte items including eggs and bacon (only after 8:45), adding up to the priciest breakfast in town (likely to total €10). It's run by Massimo and Carmen (Thu-Tue 7:00-24:00, closed Wed, tel. 0187-821-149). If you're awaiting a train any time of day, the Blue Marlin's outdoor seating beats the platform.

Il Pirata delle Cinque Terre is located at the top of the town, where the dynamic Sicilian duo Gianluca and Massimo (hard-working twins, a.k.a. the Cannoli brothers) enthusiastically offer a great assortment of handcrafted authentic Sicilian pastries. Their fun and playful service makes up for the lack of a view. Gianluca is a pastry artist, hand-painting fanciful sculptured marzipan. Their sweet pastry breakfasts are a hit, with a stunning array of hot-out-of-the-oven treats like *panzerotto* (made of ricotta, cinnamon, and vanilla, €2.50) and hot cheese and pesto bruschetta (€3). Other favorites include their *granite* (slushees made from fresh fruit), but they proudly serve no bacon and eggs (since "this is Italy"). While the atmosphere of the place seems like suburban Milan, it has a curious charisma among its customers—bringing Vernazza a wel-come bit of Sicily (daily 6:30-24:00, also simple lunches and tasty dinners, Via Gavino 36, tel. 0187-812-047).

Ananasso Bar feels Old World, with youthful energy and a great location with little tables right on the harbor. They offer toasted *panini*, pastries, and designer cappuccino. You can eat a bit cheaper at the bar (you're welcome to picnic on the nearby bench or seawall rocks with a Mediterranean view) or enjoy the best-situated tables in town (Fri-Wed 8:00-late, closed Thu).

Picnic Breakfast: Drop by one of Vernazza's several little bak-eries, focaccia shops, or grocery stores to assemble a breakfast to eat on the breakwater. Top it off with a coffee in a nearby bar.

Lunch and Dinner

If you enjoy Italian cuisine and seafood, Vernazza's restaurants are worth the splurge. All take pride in their cooking. Wander around at about 20:00 and compare the ambience, but don't wait too late to eat—many kitchens close at 22:00. To get an out-door table on summer weekends, reserve ahead. Expect to spend €10 for pastas, €12-16 for *secondi,* and €2-3 for a cover charge. Harborside restaurants and bars are easygoing. You're welcome to grab a cup of coffee or glass of wine and disappear somewhere on the breakwater, returning your glass when you're done. If you dine in Vernazza but are staying in another town, be sure to check train schedules before sitting down to eat, as trains run less frequently in the evening.

Above the Harbor, by the Castle

Ristorante al Castello is run by gracious and English-speaking Monica, her husband Massimo, kind Mario, and the rest of her family (you won't see mamma—she's busy personally cooking each home-style *secondo*). Hike high above town to just below the castle for commanding views. Their *lasagne al pesto*, "spaghetti on the rocks" (noodles with shellfish), and scampi crêpes are time-honored family specialties. For simple fare and a special evening, reserve one of the dozen romantic cliff-side sea-view tables for two. Some of these tables snake around the castle, where you'll feel like you're eating all alone with the Mediterranean. Monica offers a free *sciacchetrà* or *limoncello* with biscotti if you have this book (€10 pastas, €12 *secondi*, Thu-Tue 12:00-15:00 for lunch, 19:00-22:00 for dinner, closed Wed and Nov-April, tel. 0187-812-296).

Ristorante Belforte's experimental, beautifully presented, creative cuisine includes a hearty *zuppa Michela* (€23 for a boatload of seafood), fishy *spaghetti Bruno* (€13), and *trofie al pesto* (hand-rolled noodles with pesto). Their classic *antipasto del nostro chef* (€36 for six plates) is plenty for two people. From the breakwater, follow either the stairs or the rope that leads up and around to the restaurant. You'll find a tangle of tables embedded in four levels of the lower part of the old castle. For the ultimate seaside perch, call and reserve one of four tables on the *terrazza con vista* (view terrace). Most of Belforte's seating is outdoors—if the weather's bad, the interior can get crowded (€15 pastas, €23 *secondi*, €3 cover, Wed-Mon 12:00-15:00 & 19:00-22:00, closed Tue and Nov-March, tel. 0187-812-222, Michela).

Harborside

Gambero Rosso ("Red Prawn," the same name as Italy's top restaurant guide) is considered Vernazza's most venerable restaurant. It feels dressy and costs more than the others. Try Chef Claudio's namesake risotto (€15 pastas, €20 *secondi*, €3 cover, Tue-Sun 12:00-15:00 & 19:00-22:00, closed Mon and Dec-Feb, Piazza Marconi 7, tel. 0187-812-265).

Trattoria del Capitano serves *spaghetti con frutti di mare* (pasta entangled with various types of seafood) and *grigliata mista* (a mix of seasonal Mediterranean fish) among their offerings (€10 pastas, €16 *secondi*, €2 cover, Wed-Mon 12:00-15:00 & 19:00-22:00, closed Tue except in Aug, closed Nov-Dec, tel. 0187-812-201, while Paolo and Eduardo speak English, grandpa Giacomo doesn't need to).

Trattoria Gianni is an old standby for locals and tourists who appreciate the best prices on the harbor. You'll enjoy well-prepared seafood and receive steady, reliable, and friendly service from Emanuele and Alessandro. Ask about "off-menu specials." While the outdoor seating is basic, the indoor setting is classy (€15 pastas, €15 *secondi*, €3 cover, check their *menù cucina tipica Vernazza*, Thu-Tue 12:00-15:00 & 19:00-22:00, closed Wed except July-Aug, tel. 0187-812-228).

Ristorante Pizzeria Vulnetia is simpler, serving regional specialties such as prizewinning *tegame alla Vernazza*—anchovies, tomatoes, and potatoes baked in the oven (€8 pizzas, €12 pastas, €16 *secondi*, €2 cover, Tue-Sun 12:00-15:30 & 18:30-22:00, closed Thu, Piazza Marconi 29, tel. 0187-821-193, Giuliano).

Inland, on or near the Main Street

Several of Vernazza's inland eateries manage to compete without the harbor ambience, but with slightly cheaper prices.

Trattoria da Sandro, on the main drag, mixes Genovese and Ligurian cuisine with friendly service. It can be a peaceful alternative to the harborside scene, plus they dish up award-winning stuffed mussels (€13 pastas, €15 *secondi*, Wed-Mon 12:00-15:00 & 18:30-22:00, closed Tue, Via Roma 62, tel. 0187-812-223, Gabriella and Alessandro).

Antica Osteria il Baretto is another solid bet for homey, reasonably priced traditional cuisine, run by Simone and Jenny. As it's off the harbor and a little less glitzy than the others, it's favored by locals who prefer less noisy English while they eat great homemade fish ravioli. Sitting deep in their interior can be a peaceful escape (€12 pasta, €14 *secondi*, Tue-Sat 12:00-15:00 & 19:00-22:00, closed Mon, indoor and outdoor seating, Via Roma 31).

Ristorante Incadase da Piva is a rare bit of old Vernazza. For 25 years, charismatic Piva has been known for his *tegame alla Vernazza*, his *risotto con frutti di mare* (seafood risotto), and his love of music. The town troubadour, he often serenades his guests when the cooking's done (€13 pastas, €16 *secondi*, Fri-Wed 10:30-15:00 & 18:00-22:30, closed Thu, tucked away 20 yards off the main drag, up a lane behind the pharmacy).

Other Eating Options

Il Pirata delle Cinque Terre, popular for breakfast, is also a favorite for lunch and dinner (€9 pastas, great salads, Sicilian specialties), and its homemade desserts and drinks. The Cannoli twins entertain while they serve, as diners enjoy delicious meals while laughing out loud in this simple café/pastry shop. The menu offers a break from the predictable Ligurian fare, and the bread is literally hot out of the oven (at the top of town; for complete description, see listing under "Breakfast," earlier).

Bar Baia Saracena ("Saracen Bay") serves decent pizza and microwaved pastas out on the breakwater. Eat here for the economy and the view (€5-7 salads, €9 pizza, tel. 0187-812-113, Luca).

Pizzerias, Sandwiches, and Groceries: Vernazza's main street creatively fills tourists' needs. Two pizzerias stay busy, and while they mostly do take-out, each will let you sit and eat for the same cheap price. One has tables on the street, and the other **(Ercole)** hides a tiny terrace and a few tables out back (it's the only pizzeria in town with a wood-fired oven). **Forno Bakery** has good focaccia and veggie tarts, and several bars sell sandwiches and pizza by the slice. **Grocery stores** also make inexpensive sandwiches to order (generally Mon-Sat 8:00-13:00 & 17:00-19:30, closed Sun). Tiny jars of pesto spread give elegance to picnics.

Gelato: The town's three *gelaterias* are good. What looks like **Gelateria Amore Mio** (near the grotto, mid-town), is actually Gelateria Stalin—founded in 1968 by a pastry chef with that unfortunate name. His niece Sonia, who speaks "ice cream," and nephew Francesco now run the place, and are generous with free tastes. They have a neat little licking zone with tiny benches hidden above the crowds; look for it on the little bridge a few steps past their door. They also have good coffee (daily 8:00-24:00, closes at 19:00 off-season, 24 flavors, sit there or take it to go).

Monterosso al Mare (Town #5)

This is a resort with a few cars and lots of hotels, rentable beach umbrellas, crowds, and a little more late-night action than the

neighboring towns. Monterosso al Mare—the only Cinque Terre town built on flat land—has two parts: A new town (called Fegina) with a parking lot, train station, and TI; and an old town (Centro Storico), which cradles Old World charm in its small, crooked lanes. In the old town, you'll find hole-in-the-wall shops, pastel townscapes, and a new generation of creative small-businesspeople eager to keep their visitors happy.

A pedestrian tunnel connects the old with the new—but take a small detour around the point for a nicer walk. It offers a close-up view of two sights: a 16th-century lookout tower, built after the last serious pirate raid in 1545; and a Nazi "pillbox," a small, low concrete bunker where gunners hid. (During World War II, nearby La Spezia was an important Axis naval base, and Monterosso was bombed while the Germans were here.)

Strolling the waterfront promenade, you can pick out each of the Cinque Terre towns decorating the coast. After dark, they sparkle. Monterosso is the most enjoyable of the five for young travelers wanting to connect with others looking for a little evening action. Even so, Monterosso is not a full-blown Portofino-style resort—and locals appreciate quiet, sensitive guests.

Orientation to Monterosso

Tourist Information

The TI Proloco is next to the train station (April-Oct daily 9:00-19:00, closed Nov-March, exit station and go left a few doors, tel. 0187-817-506, www.prolocomonterosso.it, Annamaria). If you arrive late on a summer day, head to the Internet café for tourist information.

Arrival in Monterosso

By Train: Train travelers arrive in the new town, from which it's a scenic, flat 10-minute stroll to all the old-town action (leave station to the left; to reach hotels in the new town, turn right out of station). The bar at track 1, which overlooks the beach, is a handy place to wait while waiting for your train to pull in.

Shuttle buses run roughly hourly along the waterfront between the old town (Piazza Garibaldi, just beyond the tunnel), the train station, and the parking lot at the end of Via Fegina (*Campo Sportivo* stop). While the buses can be convenient—saving you a 10-minute schlep with your bags—they only go once an hour, and are likely not worth the trouble (€1.50, free with Cinque Terre Park Card).

The other alternative is to take a **taxi** (certain vehicles have permission to drive in the old city center). They usually wait outside the train station, but you may have to call (€7 from station to the old town, mobile 335-616-5842 or 335-628-0933).

By Car: Monterosso is 30 minutes off the freeway (exit: Levanto-Carrodano). Note that about three miles above Monterosso, a fork directs you to either *Centro Storico* (old part of town—Via Roma parking lot with a few spots, and possibly the new Loreto garage) or *Fegina* (the new town and beachfront parking, most likely where you want to go). At this point you must choose which area, because you can't drive directly from the new town to the old center (which is closed to cars without special permits).

Parking is easy (except July-Aug and summer weekends) in the huge beachfront guarded lot in the new town (€14/24 hours). If you're heading to the old town, you'll find the lot on Via Roma, a 10-minute downhill walk to the main square (€1.70/hour, €18/24 hours in the parking structure). The big, new Loreto parking garage at the top of the old town should be open in 2012.

For the cheapest Monterosso rates, park along the blue lines (5 minutes farther uphill from Via Roma parking structure) for €8 per day. See "Cinque Terre Connections" at the end of this chapter for directions from Milan and tips on driving in the Cinque Terre.

Helpful Hints

Medical Help: The town's bike-riding, leather bag-toting, English-speaking physician is **Dr. Vitone,** who charges €50-80 for a simple visit (less for poor students, mobile 338-853-0949).

Internet Access: The Net, a few steps off the main drag (Via Roma), has 10 high-speed computers (€1.50/10 minutes) and Wi-Fi. Enzo happily provides information on the Cinque Terre, has a line on local accommodations, and can burn your photos onto a DVD for €6 (daily 9:30-23:00, off-season closes for lunch and dinner breaks, Via Vittorio Emanuele 55, tel. 0187-817-288, mobile 335-778-5085, www.monterossonet .com).

Baggage Storage: Lucia's Lavarapido, two blocks from the station, provides a wonderful bag-check service—just drop off your bag for €5 (see details in next listing).

Laundry: For full-service laundry in the new town, **Lucia's Lavarapido** will return your laundry to your hotel (€12/13 pounds, daily 8:30-22:00, Via Molinelli 17, mobile 339-484-0940, Lucia and Ivano). For self-service in the old town, **Wash and Dry Lavanderia** is new and modern (€6/wash and dry, daily 7:30-23:30, Via Roma 43).

Massage: Giorgio Moggia, the local physiotherapist, gives good massages at your hotel or in his studio (€60/hour, tel. 339-314-6127, giomogg@tin.it).

Self-Guided Walk

Welcome to Monterosso

• *Hike out from the dock in the old town and climb five rough steps to the very top of the concrete...*

Breakwater: If you're visiting by boat, you'll start here anyway. From this point, you can survey Monterosso's old town and new town (stretching to the left, with train station and parking lot), and actually see all *cinque* of the *terre* from one spot: Vernazza, Corniglia (above the shore), Manarola, and a few buildings of Riomaggiore beyond that. The little fort above, which dates from 1550, is now a private home.

These days, the harbor hosts more paddleboats than fishing boats. Sand erosion is a major problem. The partial breakwater is designed to save the beach from washing away. While old-timers remember a vast beach, their grandchildren truck in sand each spring to give tourists something to lie on. (The Nazis liked the Cinque Terre, too—find two of their bomb-hardened bunkers, near left and far right.)

The fancy €300-a-night, four-star Hotel Porto Roca (on the far right) marks the trail to Vernazza. High above, you see an example

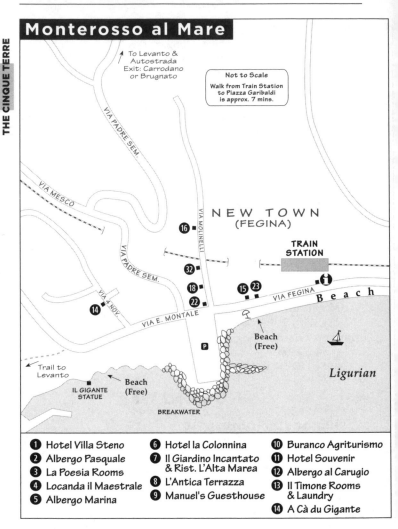

Monterosso al Mare

To Levanto &
Autostrada
Exit: Carrodano
or Brugnato

Not to Scale

Walk from Train Station
to Piazza Garibaldi
is approx. 7 mins.

VIA PADRE SEM.

VIA MESCO

VIA MOLINELLI

NEW TOWN
(FEGINA)

TRAIN
STATION

VIA PADRE SEM.

VIA 4 NOV.

VIA E. MONTALE

VIA FEGINA

Beach

Beach
(Free)

Ligurian

Trail to
Levanto

Beach
(Free)

IL GIGANTE
STATUE

BREAKWATER

1 Hotel Villa Steno
2 Albergo Pasquale
3 La Poesia Rooms
4 Locanda il Maestrale
5 Albergo Marina

6 Hotel la Colonnina
7 Il Giardino Incantato
& Rist. L'Alta Marea
8 L'Antica Terrazza
9 Manuel's Guesthouse

10 Buranco Agriturismo
11 Hotel Souvenir
12 Albergo al Carugio
13 Il Timone Rooms
& Laundry
14 A Cà du Gigante

of the costly roads built in the 1980s to connect the Cinque Terre towns with the freeway over the hills. The two capes (Punta di Montenero and Punta Mesco) define the Cinque Terre region. The closer cape, Punta Mesco, marks an important sea-life sanctuary, home to a rare sea grass that provides an ideal home for fish eggs. Buoys keep fishing boats away. The cape was once a quarry, providing employment to locals who chipped out the stones used to build the local towns (the green stones making up part of the breakwater below you are from there).

On the far end of the new town, marking the best free beach around, you can just see the statue named *Il Gigante*. It's 45 feet tall

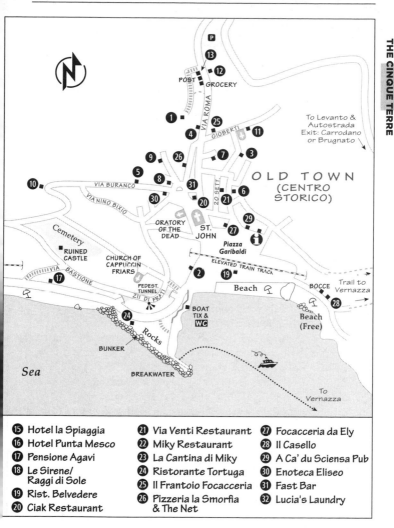

15 Hotel la Spiaggia
16 Hotel Punta Mesco
17 Pensione Agavi
18 Le Sirene/
    Raggi di Sole
19 Rist. Belvedere
20 Ciak Restaurant

21 Via Venti Restaurant
22 Miky Restaurant
23 La Cantina di Miky
24 Ristorante Tortuga
25 Il Frantoio Focacceria
26 Pizzeria la Smorfia
    & The Net

27 Focacceria da Ely
28 Il Casello
29 A Ca' du Sciensa Pub
30 Enoteca Eliseo
31 Fast Bar
32 Lucia's Laundry

and once held a trident. While it looks as if it were hewn from the rocky cliff, it's actually made of reinforced concrete and dates from the beginning of the 20th century, when it supported a dancing terrace for a *fin de siècle* villa. A violent storm left the giant holding nothing but memories of Monterosso's glamorous age.

• *From the breakwater, walk into the old-town square (just under the train tracks and to the right). Find the statue of a dandy holding what looks like a box cutter in...*

Piazza Garibaldi: The statue honors Giuseppe Garibaldi, the dashing firebrand revolutionary who, in the 1860s, helped unite the people of Italy into a modern nation. Facing Garibaldi, with your back to the sea, you'll see (from right to left) the City Hall (with the now-required European Union flag beside the Italian one) and a big home and recreation center for poor and homeless elderly. You'll also see A Ca' du Sciensa pub (with historic town photos inside and upstairs; you're welcome to pop in for a look—see "Nightlife in Monterosso," later).

Just under the bell tower (with your back to the sea, it's on your left), a set of covered arcades facing the sea is where the old-timers hang out (they see all and know all). The crenellated bell tower marks the church.

• Go to church (the entrance is on the inland side).

Church of St. John the Baptist (Chiesa di San Giovanni Battista): This black-and-white church, with white marble from Carrara and green marble from Punte Mesco, is typical of this region's Romanesque style. Note the lacy, stone rose window above the entrance. It's as delicate as crochet work, with 18 slender mullions (the petals of the rose). The marble stripes get narrower the higher they go, creating the illusion of a church that's taller than it really is. Step inside for more Ligurian Gothic: original marble columns and capitals with pointed arches to match. The octagonal baptismal font (in the back of the church) was carved from Carrara marble in 1359. Imagine the job getting that from the quarries to here. Nearby is a wooden statue of St. Anthony, carved about 1400, which once graced a church that stood atop Punta Mesco. The church itself dates from 1307—see the proud inscription on the middle column inside: "MilleCCCVII." Outside the church, on the side facing the main street, find the high-water mark from a November 1966 flood (the same month as the flood that devastated Florence).

• Leaving the church, immediately turn left and go to church again.

Oratory of the Dead (Oratorio dei Neri): During the Counter-Reformation, the Catholic Church offset the rising influence of the Lutherans by creating brotherhoods of good works. These religious Rotary clubs were called "confraternities." Monterosso had two, nicknamed White and Black. This building is the oratory of the Black group, whose mission—as the macabre decor filling the interior indicates—was to arrange for funerals and take care of widows, orphans, the shipwrecked, and the souls of those who ignore the request for a €1 donation. It dates from the 16th century, and membership has passed from father to son for generations. Notice the fine carved choir stalls (c. 1700) just inside the door, and the haunted-house chandeliers. Look up at the ceiling to find the symbol of the confraternity: a skull-and-crossbones and an hourglass...death awaits us all.

• Return to the beach and find the brick steps that lead up to the hill-capping convent (starting between the train tracks and the pedestrian *tunnel). Stop above the castle at a statue of St. Francis and a wolf taking in a grand view. Enjoy another opportunity to see all five of the Cinque Terre towns. From here, backtrack 20 yards and continue uphill.*

The Switchbacks of the Friars: Follow the yellow brick road (OK, it's orange...but I couldn't help singing as I skipped skyward). Climb uphill until you reach a convent church, then a cemetery, in a ruined castle at the summit. The lane *(Salita dei Cappuccini)* is nicknamed *Zii di Frati* ("switchbacks of the friars").

• *When you reach a gate marked* Convento e Chiesa Cappuccini, *you have arrived.*

Church of the Capuchin Friars: The former convent is now manned by a single caretaker friar. Before stepping inside, notice the church's striped Romanesque facade. It's all fake. Tap it—no marble, just cheap 18th-century stucco. Sit in the rear pew. The high altarpiece painting of St. Francis can be rolled up on special days to reveal a statue of Mary standing behind it. Look at the statue of St. Anthony to the right and smile (you're on convent camera). Wave at the security camera—they're nervous about the precious painting to your left.

This fine painting of the Crucifixion is attributed to Anthony van Dyck, the 17th-century Flemish master who lived and worked for years in nearby Genoa (though art historians suspect that, at best, it was painted by someone in the artist's workshop). When Jesus died, the earth went dark. Notice the eclipsed sun in the painting, just to the right of the cross. Do the electric candles work? Pick one up, pray for peace, and plug it in. (Leave €0.50, or unplug it and put it back.)

• *Leave and turn left to hike 100 yards uphill to the cemetery that fills the remains of the castle, capping the hill. Look out from the gate and enjoy the view.*

Cemetery in the Ruined Castle: In the Dark Ages, the village huddled within this castle. Slowly it expanded. Notice the town view from here—no sea. You're looking at the oldest part of Monterosso, huddled behind the hill, out of view of 13th-century pirates. Explore the cemetery, but remember that cemeteries are sacred and treasured places (as is clear by the abundance of fresh flowers). Ponder the black-and-white photos of grandparents past. *Q.R.P.* is *Qui Riposa in Pace* (a.k.a. R.I.P.). Rich families had their own little tomb buildings. Climb to the very summit—the castle's keep, or place of last refuge. Priests are buried in a line of graves closest to the sea, but facing inland, toward the town's holy sanctuary high on the hillside (above the road, with its triangular steeple peeking above the trees). Each Cinque Terre town has a lofty sanctuary, dedicated to Mary and dear to the village hearts.

• *From here, your tour is over—any trail leads you back into town.*

Sights in Monterosso

Beaches—Monterosso's beaches, immediately in front of the train station, are easily the Cinque Terre's best and most crowded. This town is a sandy resort with rentable beach extras: Figure €20 to rent two chairs and an umbrella for the day. Light lunches are served by beach cafés to sunbathers at their lounge chairs. It's often worth the euros to enjoy a private beach. If you see umbrellas on a beach, it means you'll have to pay a rental fee; otherwise the sand is free (all the beaches are marked on this book's Monterosso al Mare map). Don't use your white hotel towels; most hotels will give you beach towels—sometimes for a fee. The local hidden beach, which is free, gravelly, and generally less crowded, is tucked away under Il Casello restaurant at the east end of town, near the trailhead to Vernazza. The bocce ball court (next to Il Casello) is busy with the old boys enjoying their favorite pastime.

Kayaks—**Samba** rents kayaks on the beach (€7/hour for 1-person kayak, €12/hour for 2-person kayak, to the right of train station as you exit, mobile 339-681-2265, Domenico). The paddle to Vernazza is a favorite.

Shuttle Buses for High-Country Hikes—Monterosso's bus service (described earlier, under "Arrival in Monterosso") continues beyond the town limits, but check the schedules—only one or two departures a day head into the high country. Some buses go to the Sanctuary of Our Lady of Soviore, from where you can hike back down to Monterosso (1.5 hours, moderately steep). Rides cost €1.50 (free with Cinque Terre Park Card, pick up schedule from park office). Or you can hike to Levanto (no Cinque Terre Park card necessary, not as stunning as the rest of the coastal trail, 2.5 hours, straight uphill and then easy decline, follow signs at west end of the new town). For hiking details, ask at the train station TI.

Wine-Tasting—Buranco Agriturismo offers visits to their vineyard and cantina daily at 12:00. You'll taste two of their wines plus a grappa and a *limoncino,* along with home-cooked food (€25/person with snacks, €40/person for full lunch, reservations advised at least three days in advance, English may be limited, follow Via Buranco uphill to path, 10 minutes above town, tel. 0187-817-677, www.burancocinqueterre.it). They also rent apartments; see "Sleeping in Monterosso," later.

Boat Rides—From the old-town harbor, boats run nearly hourly (10:30-17:00) to Vernazza, Manarola, Riomaggiore, and Portovenere. Schedules are posted in Cinque Terre park offices.

Nightlife in Monterosso

A Ca' du Sciensa has nothing to do with science—it's the last name of the town moneybags who owned this old mansion. The antique dumbwaiter is still in use—a remnant from the days when servants toiled downstairs while the big shots wined and dined up top. This classy yet laid-back pub offers breezy square seating, bar action on the ground level, an intimate lounge upstairs, and discreet balconies overlooking the square to share with your best travel buddy. It's a good place for light meals from a fun and accessible menu: €5-6 sandwiches, salads, and microwaved pastas. They offer €6 cocktails and mojitos with free *aperitivo* snacks from 17:30 to 20:30. Luca welcomes you to wander around the place and view the old Cinque Terre photo collection (daily 10:00-24:00, closed Nov-March, Piazza Garibaldi 17, tel. 0187-818-233).

Enoteca Eliseo, the first (and I'd say best) wine bar in town, comes with operatic ambience. Eliseo and his wife, Mary, love music and wine. You can select a fine bottle from their shop shelf, and for €7 extra, enjoy it and the village action from their cozy tables. If you've ever wanted an education in grappa, talk to Eliseo—he stocks 96 varieties. Wines sold by the glass *(bicchiere)* are posted (Wed-Mon 9:00-24:00, closed Tue, Piazza Matteotti 3, a block inland behind church, tel. 0187-817-308).

Fast Bar, the best bar in town for young travelers and night owls, is located on Via Roma in the old town. Customers mix travel tales with big, cold beers, and the crowd (and the rock 'n' roll) gets noisier as the night rolls on. Come here to watch Italian or American sporting events on TV any time of day (sandwiches and snacks usually served until midnight, open nightly until 2:00, closed Nov-March, Alex, Francisco, and Stefano).

La Cantina di Miky, in the new town just beyond the train station, is a trendy bar-restaurant with an extensive cocktail and grappa menu. The seating is in three zones: overlooking the beach, in the garden, or in the cellar. Run by Manuel, son of well-known local restaurateur Miky, it sometimes hosts live music. Manuel offers a fun "five villages" wine-tasting with local meats and cheeses (daily until well after 24:00, Via Fegina 90, tel. 0187-802-525).

Sleeping in Monterosso

(€1 = about $1.40, country code: 39)
Monterosso, the most beach-resorty of the five Cinque Terre towns, offers maximum comfort and ease. The TI Proloco just outside the train station can give you a list of €70-80 double rooms. Rooms in Monterosso are a better value for your money than similar rooms in crowded Vernazza, and the proprietors seem more

genuine and welcoming. To locate the hotels, see the Monterosso al Mare map.

In the Old Town

$$$ Hotel Villa Steno is lovingly managed and features great view balconies, panoramic gardens with sun beds, air-conditioning, and the friendly help of English-speaking Matteo and his wife, Carla. Of their 16 rooms, 12 have view balconies (Sb-€110, Db-€170, Tb-€195, Qb-€225, includes hearty buffet breakfast, €10 per night discount with cash and this book in 2012, Internet access and Wi-Fi, laundry, parking-€8—reserve in advance, Via Roma 109, tel. 0187-817-028 or 0187-818-336, fax 0187-817-354, www.villa steno.com, steno@pasini.com). It's a 15-minute hike (or €8 taxi ride) from the train station to the top of the old town. Readers get a free Cinque Terre info packet and a glass of the local sweet wine, *sciacchetrà*, when they check in—ask for it.

$$$ Albergo Pasquale is a modern, comfortable place with 15 rooms, run by the same family as the Hotel Villa Steno (above). It's conveniently located just a few steps from the beach, boat dock, tunnel entrance to the new town, and train tracks. While there is some traffic and train noise, it's mostly a lullaby of waves. Located right on the harbor, it has an elevator and offers easier access than most (same prices and welcome drink as Villa Steno; air-con, all rooms with sea view, Via Fegina 8, tel. 0187-817-550 or 0187-817-477, fax 0187-817-056, www.hotelpasquale.com, pasquale@pasini .com, Felicita and Marco).

$$$ La Poesia has four warmly colored rooms that share a peaceful garden terrace, where you'll enjoy a complimentary *aperitivo* upon arrival (Db-€150, suite-€40 extra, small discount for multi-night stays, air-con, Via Genova 4, tel. 0187-817-283, www .lapoesia-cinqueterre.com, info@lapoesia-cinqueterre.com, mamma Nicoletta speaks little English, daughter Veronica speaks more).

$$$ Locanda il Maestrale rents six small, stylish rooms in a sophisticated and peaceful little inn. Although renovated with all the modern comforts, it retains centuries-old character under frescoed ceilings. Its peaceful sun terrace overlooking the old town and Via Roma action is a delight (small Db-€115, Db-€145, suite-€170, less off-season, 10 percent discount with cash and this book, air-con, Wi-Fi, Via Roma 37, tel. 0187-817-013, mobile 338-4530-531, fax 0187-817-084, www.locandamaestrale.net, maestrale @monterossonet.com, Stefania).

$$$ Albergo Marina, creatively run by enthusiastic husband-and-wife team Marina and Eraldo, has 23 thoughtfully appointed rooms and a garden with lemon trees. With a free and filling buffet featuring local specialties from 14:00 to 17:00 daily, they offer a fine value (standard Db-€130, 10 percent discount with cash and this book in 2012, elevator, air-con, Wi-Fi, free use of kayak and snorkel equipment, Via Buranco 40, tel. 0187-817-613, fax 0187-817-242, www.hotelmarina5terre.com, marina@hotelmarina5terre.com).

$$$ Hotel la Colonnina, a comfy, modern place with 21 big and pretty rooms, is buried in the town's fragrant and sleepy back streets with no sea views (Db-€142, Tb-€200, Qb-€225, €15 more for bigger rooms with viewless terrace, cash only, air-con, Internet access and Wi-Fi, fridges, elevator, inviting rooftop terrace with sun beds, garden, Via Zuecca 6, tel. 0187-817-439, fax 0187-817-788, www.lacolonninacinqueterre.it, info@lacolonninacinqueterre.it, Christina). The hotel is in the old town behind the statue of Garibaldi (take street to left of A Ca' du Sciensa one block up).

$$$ Il Giardino Incantato ("The Enchanted Garden") is a charming four-room B&B in a tastefully renovated 16th-century Ligurian home in the heart of the old town. Breakfast is served in a hidden garden, which is illuminated with candles in the evening (Db-€170, Db suite-€200, air-con, free minibar and tea and coffee service, Via Mazzini 18, tel. 0187-818-315, mobile 333-264-9252, www.ilgiardinoincantato.net, giardino_incantato@libero.it, kind and eager-to-please Fausto and Mariapia).

$$$ L'Antica Terrazza rents four classy rooms right in town. With a pretty terrace overlooking the pedestrian street and minimal stairs, Raffaella and John offer a good deal (Db-€110, 5 percent discount with cash, air-con, Internet access and Wi-Fi, Vicolo San Martino 1, tel. 0187-817-499, mobile 347-132-6213, www.antica terrazza.com, post@anticaterrazza.com).

$$$ Manuel's Guesthouse, perched among terraces, is a garden getaway ruled by disheveled artist Manuel and run by his nephew Lorenzo. They have seven big, bright rooms and a grand view. Their killer terrace is hard to leave—especially after a few drinks (Db-€100, big Db with grand-view balcony-€120, prices good with this book, cash only, air-con, Internet access and Wi-Fi, in old town, up about 100 steps behind church at top of town, Via San Martino 39, mobile 333-439-0809 or 329-547-3775, www.manuelsguesthouse.com, info@manuelsguesthouse.com).

$$$ Buranco Agriturismo, a 10-minute walk from the old town, has wonderful gardens and views over the vine-covered valley. Its primary business is wine and olive-oil production, but they offer three apartments at a good price. It's a rare opportunity to stay in a farmhouse but still be able to get to town on foot (2-6 people-€60/person including breakfast, €30/child under 12, dinner on request, air-con, free shuttle from station, open year-round, tel. 0187-817-677, mobile 349-434-8046, fax 0187-802-084, www.burancocinqueterre.it, info@buranco.it, informally run by Loredana, Mary, and Giulietta).

$$ Hotel Souvenir is Monterosso's cash-only backpacker hotel. It has 30 rooms in two buildings, each utilitarian but comfortable (one more stark than the other). Both share a lounge and pleasant leafy courtyard. The basic one is popular with students (S-€30, Sb-€35, D-€55, Db-€70, T-€105, breakfast-€5); the other is nicer and pricier (Sb-€45, Db-€80, Tb-€120, includes breakfast; walk three blocks inland from the main old-town square to Via Gioberti 24, tel. 0187-817-822, tel. & fax 0187-817-595, hotel _souvenir@yahoo.com, Beppe).

$$ Albergo al Carugio is a simple, practical nine-room place in a big apartment-style building at the top of the old town. It's quiet, comfy, and functional (Db-€75-80, air-con, Wi-Fi, Via Roma 100, tel. 0187-817-453, www.alcarugio.it, info@alcarugio.it, Andrea and Simona).

$$ Il Timone Rooms, a little B&B by the post office, has three tidy, modern rooms. Francesco also rents a few rooms near the cemetery, but they aren't worth the hike (Db-€90, breakfast at a bar, air-con, Wi-Fi, Via Roma 75, tel. 349-870-8666, www .iltimonedimonterosso.it).

In the New Town

$$$ A Cà du Gigante, despite its name, is a tiny yet stylish refuge with nine rooms. About 100 yards from the beach (and surrounded by blocky apartments on a modern street), the interior is tastefully done with modern comfort in mind (Db-€160, Db sea-view suite-€180, 10 percent discount with 3-night stay and this book in 2012, occasional last-minute deals, air-con, free parking, Via IV Novembre 11, tel. 0187-817-401, fax 0187-817-375, www.ilgigante cinqueterre.it, gigante@ilgigantecinqueterre.it, Claudia).

$$$ Hotel la Spiaggia is a venerable old 19-room place facing the beach and run with attitude by Poggi Andrea and his gentle daughter Maria. Half of the rooms come with air-con and half with sea views, but all are the same price—request what you like when you reserve (Db-€160, €10 discount for 2-night stays, includes breakfast and parking, elevator, Via Lungomare 98, tel. 0187-817-567, fax 0187-817-075, www.laspiaggiahotel.com, hotel laspiaggia@libero.it).

$$$ Hotel Punta Mesco is a tidy, well-run little haven renting 17 quiet, modern rooms. While none have views, 10 rooms have small terraces. For the price, it may offer the best comfort in town (Db-€132, Tb-€170, 5 percent discount with cash, air-con, Wi-Fi, free loaner bikes, free parking, Via Molinelli 35, tel. & fax 0187-817-495, www.hotelpuntamesco.it, info@hotelpuntamesco.it, Diego and Anna).

$$$ Pensione Agavi has 10 spartan, hostel-like, overpriced rooms, about half overlooking the beach near the big rock. This is not a place to party—it feels like an old hospital with narrow hall-ways (D-€80, Db-€110, Tb-€140, same price with or without view, 10 percent discount for 2 nights or more, no breakfast, cash only, refrigerators, turn left out of station to Fegina 30, tel. 0187-817-171, mobile 333-697-4071, fax 0187-818-264, hotel.agavi@libero.it, Hillary).

$ Le Sirene/Raggi di Sole, with nine simple rooms in two humble buildings, is about the cheapest place in town. It's run from a hole-in-the-wall reception desk a block from the station, just off the water. I'd request the Le Sirene building, which doesn't have train noise and is a bit nicer than Raggi di Sole (Db-€80, third person-€40, fans, Via Molinelli 10, mobile 393-935-7683, www.sirenerooms.com, sirenerooms@gmail.com, Ermanna).

Eating in Monterosso

Restaurants

Ristorante Belvedere, big and sprawling, is *the* place for a good-value meal indoors or outdoors on the harborfront. Their *amfora belvedere*—mixed seafood stew—is huge, and can easily be split among up to four diners (€45). Share with your group and add pasta for a fine meal. Mussel fans will enjoy the *tagliolini della casa* (€8). It's energetically run by Federico and Roberto (€9 pastas, €12 *secondi*, €2 cover, Wed-Mon 12:00-14:30 & 19:00-22:00, usually closed Tue, on the harbor in the old town, tel. 0187-817-033).

L'Alta Marea offers special fish ravioli, the catch of the day, and huge crocks of fresh, steamed mussels. Young chef Marco cooks with charisma, while his wife, Anna, takes good care of the guests. This place is quieter, buried in the old town two blocks off the beach, and has covered tables out front for people-watching. This is a good opportunity to try rabbit (€9 pastas and pizza, €12-15 *secondi*, €2 cover, 10 percent discount with cash and this book in 2012, Thu-Tue 12:00-15:00 & 18:00-22:00, closed Wed, Via Roma 54, tel. 0187-817-170).

Ciak—high-energy and tightly packed—is a local institution with reliably good food and higher prices. It's known for its huge, sizzling terra-cotta crock for two crammed with the day's catch and accompanied by risotto or spaghetti, or served swimming in a soup *(zuppa).* Another popular choice is the seafood *antipasto Lampara.* Stroll a couple of paces past the outdoor tables up Via Roma to see what Ciak has on the stove (Thu-Tue 12:00-15:00 & 19:00-22:30, closed Wed, tel. 0187-817-014).

Via Venti is a quiet little trattoria, hidden in an alley deep in the heart of the old town, where Papa Ettore creates imaginative seafood dishes using the day's catch and freshly made pasta. Ilaria and her partner Michele serve up delicate and savory gnocchi (tiny potato dumplings) with crab sauce, tender ravioli stuffed with fresh fish, and pear-and-cheese pasta. There's nothing pretentious here... just good cooking, service, and prices (€11 pastas, €16 *secondi,* Fri-Wed 12:00-15:00 & 18:30-22:30, closed Thu, tel. 0187-818-347). From the bottom of Via Roma, with your back to the sea and the church to your left, head to the right down Via XX Settembre and follow it to the end, to #32.

Miky is packed with well-dressed locals who know their seafood and want to eat it in a classy environment without spending a fortune. For elegantly presented, top-quality food, this is my Cinque Terre favorite. It's clearly a proud family operation: Miky (dad), Simonetta (mom), and charming Sara (daughter, who greets guests) all work hard. All their pasta is "pizza pasta"—cooked normally but finished in a bowl that's encased in a thin pizza crust. They cook the concoction in a wood-fired oven to keep in the aroma. Miky's has a fine wine list with many available by the glass if you ask. If I were ever to require a dessert, it would be their mixed sampler plate, *dolce mista*—€10 and plenty for two (€15 pastas, €22 *secondi,* €8 sweets, Wed-Mon 12:00-15:00 & 19:00-23:00, closed Tue, reservations wise in summer, diners tend to dress up a bit, in the new town 100 yards north of train station at Via Fegina 104, tel. 0187-817-608).

La Cantina di Miky, a few doors down toward the station, serves Ligurian specialties (chef Boris loves anchovies) that follow in Miky's family tradition of quality (it's run by son Manuel). It's more trendy and informal than Miky's, and you can sit downstairs, in the garden, or overlooking the sea (€16 anchovy tasting plate, €13 pastas, €15 *secondi,* creative desserts, daily 12:00-24:00 or later, Via Fegina 90, tel. 0187-802-525). This place doubles as a cocktail bar in the evenings—see "Nightlife in Monterosso," earlier.

Ristorante Tortuga is the top option in Monterosso for seaview elegance, with gorgeous outdoor seating on a bluff and an elegant white-tablecloth-and-candles interior. If you're out and about, drop by to consider which table you'd like to reserve for later (€15 pastas, €20 *secondi,* Tue-Sun 12:00-14:30 & 18:00-22:00, closed Mon, just outside the tunnel that connects the old and new town, tel. 0187-800-065, mobile 333-240-7956, Silvia and Giamba).

Il Casello is the only place for a fun meal on a terrace overlooking the old-town beach. With outdoor tables on a rocky outcrop, it's a pleasant spot for a salad or a sandwich, or well-prepared pasta or *secondi* (lunch only, daily April-Oct, closed Nov-March, mobile 333-492-7629, Bacco).

Light Meals, Take-Out Food, and Breakfast

Lots of shops and bakeries sell pizza and focaccia for an easy picnic at the beach or on the trail. At **Il Frantoio,** Simone makes tasty pizza to go or to munch perched on a stool (Fri-Wed 9:00-14:00 & 16:00-19:30, closed Thu, just off Via Roma at Via Gioberti 1, tel. 0187-818-333). **Pizzeria la Smorfia** also cooks up good pizza to eat in or take out. Pizzas come in two sizes—the large can feed three (Fri-Wed 11:30-15:00 & 18:00-23:00, closed Thu, Via Vittorio Emanuele 73, tel. 0187-818-395). **Focacceria da Ely** makes airy focaccia and thick-crust pizzas for casual seating or take-out (daily 10:30-20:00, until 24:00 in summer, Emigliano).

For a quick bite right at the train station, consider **Il Massimo della Focaccia.** Massimo and Daniella serve local quiche-like tortes, sandwiches, focaccia pizzas, and desserts. With benches just in front, this is a good bet for a €4 light meal with a sea view (daily, Via Fegina 50 at the entry to the station).

Cinque Terre Connections

By Train

The five towns of the Cinque Terre are on a pokey milk-run train line. Erratically timed but roughly hourly trains connect each town with the others, plus La Spezia, Genoa, and Riviera towns to the north. While a few of these local trains go to more distant points (Milan or Pisa), it's much faster to change in La Spezia, Monterosso, or Sestri Levante to a bigger train (local train info tel. 0187-817-458, www.trenitalia.com).

From La Spezia Centrale by Train to: Rome (7/day, 3-4.5 hours, more with changes, €45; an evening train—departing around 20:00—gives you a complete day in the region while still getting you to Rome that night), **Pisa** (about hourly, 1-1.5 hours, €5), **Florence** (5/day direct, otherwise nearly hourly, 2.5 hours, €9.30), **Milan** (about hourly, 3 hours direct or with change in Genoa, €22), **Venice** (about hourly, 5-6 hours, 1-3 changes, €50).

From Monterosso by Train to: Venice (about hourly, 6-7 hours, 1-3 changes, €52), **Milan** (8/day direct, otherwise hourly with change in Genoa, 3-4 hours, €22), **Genoa** (hourly, 1.2-2 hours, €8), **Turin** (8/day, 3-4 hours, €20), **Pisa** (hourly, 1-2 hours, €6-10), **Sestri Levante** (hourly, 20-40 minutes, most trains to Genoa stop here, €3), **La Spezia** (hourly, 20-30 minutes), **Levanto** (2-3/hour, 4 minutes), **Santa Margherita Ligure** (at least hourly, 45 minutes, €2), **Rome** (hourly, 4.5 hours, change in La Spezia, €50). For destinations in **France,** change trains in Genoa.

By Car

Because these towns are close together and have frequent transportation connections, bringing a car to the Cinque Terre is not the best idea. If your plans require it, however, here are some basic tips: stay in a hotel that includes parking, use public transportation or hike between towns, and for day-trip parking, go to Monterosso (€14-18/day), Riomaggiore (€22/day), or Manarola (€15/day). Don't drive to Vernazza, as finding a spot is tough. Parking anywhere on the Cinque Terre is truly a mess in July and August.

Milan to the Cinque Terre (130 miles): Drivers speed south on autostrada A-7 from Milan, skirt Genoa, and drive a little bit of Italy's curviest and narrowest freeways, passing the Cinque Terre toward the port of La Spezia (A-12). Another option is to take the slightly straighter A-1 via the city of Parma, followed by A-15 to La Spezia. This route takes the same amount of time (about 2.5 hours), even though it covers more miles.

Coming from either direction, and for either Monterosso or Vernazza, exit autostrada A-12 at *uscita Carrodano*, northwest of La Spezia. Don't take Cinque Terre exits before Carrodano to reach these towns.

Monterosso is 30 minutes from the autostrada. Remember that the highway divides as you approach Monterosso—you must choose between the road to Centro Storico (the old town) or the one to Fegina (the new town and beachfront parking).

Vernazza is 45 minutes from the autostrada. The drive down to Vernazza is scenic, narrow, and scary, and you'll probably lose time looking for parking.

To drive to **Riomaggiore, Corniglia,** or **Manarola,** leave the freeway at La Spezia.

Within the Cinque Terre: On busy weekends, holidays, and in July and August, both Vernazza and Monterosso fill up, and police at the top of town will deny entry to anyone without a hotel reservation. It's smart to have a confirmation in hand. If you don't, insist (politely) that they allow you to enter—but only if you actually have a room reserved (the police might call your hotel to check your story).

Parking Tips: Each Cinque Terre town has a parking lot and a once-an-hour shuttle bus to get you into town (except Corniglia), though all parking areas are no more than a 10-minute walk uphill from the center.

White signs post valid hours for pay parking, which usually don't charge 24:00-8:00. Anyone can park where there are blue lines. Parking is cash only in all towns (except Riomaggiore, where some readers have been overcharged on their credit cards—best to pay in cash).

If you plan to find parking in any of the Cinque Terre towns, try to arrive between 10:00-11:00, when overnight visitors are usually departing. Or you can park your car in Levanto (see next chapter), then take the train into the town of your choice. In these bigger towns, confirm that your parking spot is OK, and leave nothing inside to steal.

A few hotels offer parking for free or a daily charge. In **Monterosso,** consider Hotel Villa Steno, A Cà du Gigante, or Hotel Punta Mesco. For **Riomaggiore,** try Locanda del Sole, Locanda Ca' dei Duxi, or Villa Argentina. In Volastra (a shuttle ride above **Manarola**), try Hotel il Saraceno. Rooms listed in this book for Corniglia and Vernazza do not offer parking.

RIVIERA TOWNS NEAR THE CINQUE TERRE

Levanto • Sestri Levante • Santa Margherita Ligure • Portofino • La Spezia • Carrara • Portovenere

The Cinque Terre is tops, but several towns to the north have a breezy beauty and more beaches. Towns to the south offer a mix of marble, trains, and yachts.

Levanto, the northern gateway to the Cinque Terre, has a long beach and a scenic, strenuous trail to Monterosso al Mare. Sestri Levante, on a narrow peninsula flanked by two beaches, is for sun-seekers. Santa Margherita Ligure is more of a real town, with actual sights, beaches, and easy connections with Portofino by trail, bus, or boat. All three towns are a straight shot to the Cinque Terre by train.

South of the Cinque Terre, you'll likely pass through the workaday town of La Spezia (don't stay here unless you're desperate), the southern gateway to the Cinque Terre. Carrara is a quickie for marble-lovers who are driving between Pisa and La Spezia. The picturesque village of Portovenere,

near La Spezia, has scenic boat connections with Cinque Terre towns.

Public transportation is the best way to get around this region. All of the places in this chapter are well connected by train and/or boat.

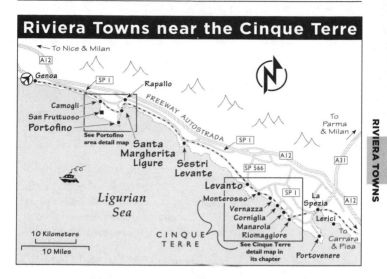

Riviera Towns near the Cinque Terre

To Nice & Milan
A12
Genoa
SP 1
Rapallo
Camogli
San Fruttuoso
Portofino
See Portofino area detail map
FREEWAY AUTOSTRADA
To Parma & Milan
Santa Margherita Ligure
Sestri Levante
SP 1
A12
SP 566
Levanto
SP 1
La Spezia
A31
A12
Monterosso
Vernazza
Corniglia
Manarola
Riomaggiore
Lerici
To Carrara & Pisa
Portovenere
See Cinque Terre detail map in its chapter
CINQUE TERRE
Ligurian Sea
10 Kilometers
10 Miles

RIVIERA TOWNS

North of the Cinque Terre

Levanto

Graced with a long, sandy beach, Levanto is packed in summer and popular with surfers. The rest of the year, it's just a small, sleepy town, with less charm and fewer tourists than the Cinque Terre. With quick connections to Monterosso (4 minutes by train), Levanto makes a decent home base if you can't snare a room in the Cinque Terre.

Levanto has a new section (with a regular grid street plan) and a twisty old town (bisected by a modern street), plus a few pedestrian streets and a castle (not tourable). From Levanto, you can take a no-wimps-allowed hike to Monterosso (2.5 hours) or hop a boat to the Cinque Terre towns and beyond.

Orientation to Levanto

Tourist Information
The helpful TI is on Piazza Mazzini (daily 9:00-13:00 & 15:00-18:00, tel. 0187-808-125, www.comune.levanto.sp.it).

Arrival in Levanto
By Train: It's a 10-minute walk from the Levanto train station to the TI in town (head down stairs in front of station, turn right, cross bridge, then follow Corso Roma to Piazza Mazzini).

By Car: Drivers can use the cheap short-term parking in the lots in front of and on either side of the train station (€6/8 hours, €9/24 hours, note that you have to pay at the machines each day—so long-term parking is difficult). Another option is the lot across the river from the hospital on the way into town (first left after the hospital, cross bridge and immediately turn left), or north of the church on Via del Mercato (free during high season, except Wed before 14:00). For long-term parking, try the lots at Piazza Mazzini or behind the TI (€15/day).

Helpful Hints

Markets: Levanto's modern covered *mercato,* which sells produce and fish, is on Via del Mercato, between the TI and train station (Mon-Sat 8:00-13:00, closed Sun). On Wednesday morning, an **open-air market** with clothes, shoes, and housewares fills the street in front of the *mercato.*

Internet Access: Try **Viaggi Beraldi** at Via Garibaldi 102 (€2/30 minutes, Mon-Sat 9:00-12:30 & 15:30-19:15, closed Sun, tel. 0187-800-818).

Baggage Storage: None is available at the station. Baggage storage is available in La Spezia, Monterosso, and possibly Santa Margherita Ligure.

Laundry: A self-service launderette stuffed with snack and drink vending machines is at Piazza Staglieno 38 (wash-€5 including soap, dry-€5, open 24 hours daily, mobile 338-701-6341).

Bike Rental: Cicli Raso North Shore rents bikes (€8-20/day depending on type of bike, daily 9:30-12:30 & 15:30-19:30, closed Sun Nov-April, Via Garibaldi 63, tel. 0187-802-511, www.cicliraso.com).

Sports Rentals: Rosa dei Venti rents kayaks, canoes, surfboards, and windsurfing equipment right on the beach (Marco mobile 349-520-7538, Nicola mobile 349-520-7538, www.levantorosa deiventi.it).

Sights in Levanto

Beach—The beach is just two blocks away from the TI. As you face the harbor, the boat dock is to your far left, and the diving center is to your far right (rental boats available at either place in summer). You can also rent a kayak or canoe on the beach, just below the east end of the Piazza Mazzini parking lot.

During the summer, three parts of the beach are free: both sides of the boat dock, and behind the TI. The rest of the beach is broken up into private sections that charge admission. You can always stroll along the beach, even through the private sections—just don't sit down. Off-season, roughly October through May, the

Levanto

1. Albergo Primavera
2. Villa Margherita
3. A Durmì Guesthouse
4. Rist. la Loggia Rooms/Rist.
5. Villa Clelia B&B
6. La Rosa dei Venti Rooms
7. Garden Hotel
8. To Erba Persa Agriturismo
9. Ostello Ospitalia del Mare
10. Osteria Tumelin
11. Da Rino Trattoria
12. Ristorante Moresco
13. Taverna Garibaldi & Bike Rental
14. La Picea Pizzeria
15. Focacceria il Falcone
16. Il Laboratorio del Pesto
17. Dimarket Supermarket
18. Crai Supermarkets (2)
19. Il Pinguino Gelateria
20. Il Porticciolo Gelateria
21. Internet Café
22. Launderette
23. Canoe & Kayak Rental

RIVIERA TOWNS

entire beach is free, and you can lay your towel anywhere you like.
Old Town and Trailhead—The old town, several blocks from the TI and beach, clusters around Piazza del Popolo. Until a few decades ago, the town's open-air market was held at the 13th-century loggia (covered set of archways) in the square. Explore the back streets.

To reach the trailhead to Monterosso: From Piazza del Popolo, head uphill to the striped church, Chiesa di Sant'Andrea (with your back to the loggia, go straight ahead—across the square and up Via Don Emanuele Toso to the church). From the church courtyard, follow the sign to the *castello* (a private residence), go under the stone arch, and continue uphill. Or, if you're coming from the seaside promenade (Via Gaetano Semenza), head under the arches and up the stairs, and follow the signs to the *castello*. Either route leads you to a sign that points you toward Punta Mesco, the rugged tip of the peninsula. From here, you can hike up to Monterosso (2.5 hours).

Hike or Bike to Bonassola—Cross the river bridge located by the TI to wander along this waterfront path, good for walking or cycling. You'll encounter shaded tunnels and two sunny beaches on the way to the small but modern town of Bonassola with its sandy beach (25 minutes by foot, 10 minutes by bike, public beaches located a minute's walk down from trail).

Sleeping in Levanto

In this popular beach town, many hotels want you to take half-pension (lunch or dinner) in summer, especially in July and August. Prices listed here are the maximum for high season (July-Aug); smaller rooms or those without views may have a lower maximum. Expect to pay €10-30 less per night for April-June and September-October, and even less for the rest of the year. The longer your stay, the greater your bargaining power. The high number of four-person rooms in Levanto makes it particularly welcoming to families who want to explore the Cinque Terre. Many hotels rent out large apartments with kitchenettes (without a half-pension requirement), and parking is free or very reasonable.

$$$ Albergo Primavera is family-run, with 17 recently redecorated, tasteful rooms—10 with balconies but no views—just a half-block from the beach. Owner Carlo is a great cook. Try dining here once during your visit (€25 fixed-price meal); let him know a couple of hours in advance if you'd like dinner (Db-€130, request a quiet room off the street, includes hearty breakfast buffet with local hams and cheeses, air-con, Internet access and Wi-Fi; parking-€8/day June-Sept, free off-season; Via Cairoli 5, tel. 0187-808-023, fax 0187-801-588, www.primaverahotel.com, info@primaverahotel.com). Friendly Carlo, cheerful Daniela, and older daughter Giuditta speak some English, and younger daughter Gloria does her homework in the dining room.

$$$ Villa Margherita is 300 yards out of town, but the shady gardens, 11 characteristic colorfully tiled rooms (some with little view terraces), and tranquility are worth the walk (Db-€160, Tb-€175, 5 percent discount with cash and this book, elevator one flight up from street level, Internet access and Wi-Fi, free parking,

---

Sleep Code

(€1 = about $1.40, country code: 39)
S = Single, **D** = Double/Twin, **T** = Triple, **Q** = Quad, **b** = bathroom, **s** = shower only. Unless otherwise noted, credit cards are accepted, English is spoken, and breakfast is included.

To help you sort easily through these listings, I've divided the accommodations into three categories based on the price for a standard double room with bath:

$$$ **Higher Priced**—Most rooms €110 or more.
 $$ **Moderately Priced**—Most rooms between €50-110.
  $ **Lower Priced**—Most rooms €50 or less.

Prices can change without notice; verify the hotel's current rates online or by email. For other updates, see www .ricksteves.com/update.

10-minute walk to town with stairs, 5-minute walk to train station, free shuttle service from station if you tell them when you'll arrive, Via Trento e Trieste 31, tel. 0187-807-212, fax 0187-803-717, mobile 328-842-6934, www.villamargherita.net, info@villamargherita .net).

$$ A Durmì is a happy little *affitta camere* (guesthouse) owned by Graziella, Gianni, and their two daughters, Elisa and Chiara. Their sunny patios, green leafy gardens, six immaculate modern new rooms, and five sunlit apartments make a welcoming place to stay (Db-€100, extra bed-€20; apartments-€150—no minimum stay required; rooms cleaned daily, breakfast-€7, air-con, power showers, Internet access and Wi-Fi, bar, parking-€5/day, Via D. Viviani 12, tel. 0187-800-823, mobile 349-105-6016, www.adurmi .it, info@adurmi.it).

$$ Ristorante la Loggia has four pleasant, cozy, summery rooms perched above the old loggia on Piazza del Popolo (Db-€70, cash only, request balcony, quieter rooms in back, two basic side-by-side apartments great for families of 4-8, air-con, free parking, Piazza del Popolo 7, tel. & fax 0187-808-107, mobile 335-641-7701, www.tigulliovino.it, Nerina).

$$ Villa Clelia B&B has six peaceful, dark, air-conditioned rooms (named for the winds—*scirocco, maestrale,* and so on) with mini-fridges and terraces in a garden courtyard just 50 yards from the sea (Db-€70-90, minimal in-room breakfast, free parking, with loggia on your left it's straight ahead at Piazza da Passano 1, tel. 0187-808-195, mobile 328-797-6403, www.villaclelia.it, info@villa clelia.it). They also have seven central apartments that economically sleep up to five (€700/week, 3-night minimum stay). B&B

rooms are cleaned daily; you're on your own at the apartments.

$$ La Rosa dei Venti is an *affitta camere* just a couple of blocks from the beach. Enthusiastic Rosanna and her son Marco rent five super-clean rooms with dark hardwood floors, comfy rugs, and a hodgepodge of seashore decor (Db-€100, Tb-€135, includes homemade breakfast and free parking, behind Enoteca Tumelin across from Piazza del Popolo, Via della Compera, tel. 0187-808-165, mobile 333-701-3213, www.larosadeiventilevanto.com, larosadeiventi1983@libero.it).

$$ Garden Hotel offers 17 simple, bright, and modern rooms, all with balconies (but most lack views due to the elevated street), a block from the beach on busy Corso Italia (Db-€115, new fifth-floor rooms with views and terraces go for Db-€140, 5 percent discount with cash and this book, lower floors closed mid-Nov-mid-March, air-con, elevator for some floors, free Internet access and Wi-Fi, free parking but not on-site—can unload bags and then park near the station, Corso Italia 6, tel. 0187-808-173, fax 0187-803-652, www.nuovogarden.com, info@nuovogarden.com, Davide and Damiano).

$$ Erba Persa Agriturismo, a rustic farmhouse run by sunny Grazia Lizza and her gardener husband Claudio, hosts cats, dogs, pet rabbits, and donkeys among their plots of organic fruits and vegetables. It's a 10-minute walk from the train station and about a 20-minute walk from town (D-€50, Db with balcony and view-€70, Tb-€80, free Internet access, free parking, free mosquitoes, Via N. S. della Guardia 21, mobile 339-400-8587 or 348-344-7695, fax 0187-801-376, www.erbapersa.it, erbapersa@alice.it).

Hostel: $ Ostello Ospitalia del Mare has 70 beds, airy rooms, an elevator, and a terrace in a well-renovated medieval palazzo a few steps from the old town (beds-€19-27 in 4-, 6-, and 8-bed rooms with private bath, Db-€70; includes breakfast, towels, and sheets; Internet access and Wi-Fi, self-service laundry-€7.50, microwave, fridge, non-members welcome, co-ed unless you strenuously object, no curfew, no lockout; office open daily April-Oct 8:00-13:00 & 16:00-20:00, until 23:00 weekend nights, slightly shorter hours off-season; may close Nov-March, Via San Nicolò 1, tel. 0187-802-562, fax 0187-803-696, www.ospitaliadelmare.it, info@ospitaliadelmare.it).

Eating in Levanto

Osteria Tumelin, a local favorite, is more expensive than other options, but has a dressy, sophisticated ambience and a wide selection of fresh seafood. Reservations are smart on weekends or if you want to dine outside (daily 12:00-14:30 & 19:00-22:00, closed

Thu Oct-May, aquarium containing giant lobster and moray eels in first dining room on the right, Via D. Grillo 32, across street from loggia, tel. 0187-808-379).

Da Rino, a small trattoria on a quiet pedestrian lane, dishes up reasonably priced fresh seafood and homemade Ligurian specialties prepared with care. Consider the grilled *totani* (squid), *pansotti con salsa di noci* (cheese ravioli with walnut sauce), and *trofie al pesto* (local pasta with pesto sauce). Dine indoors, or at one of the few outdoor tables. On busy nights, they open up a second dining room across the street (€8 pastas, €13 *secondi,* cash only, daily 19:00-22:00, closed Tue Nov-mid-March, Via Garibaldi 10, tel. 0187-813-475).

Ristorante la Loggia, next to the old loggia, makes fine gnocchi with scampi and saffron sauce. Their daily fish specials are served in a homey wood-paneled dining room or on a little terrace overlooking the square (€10 pastas, €15 *secondi,* Thu-Tue 12:30-14:00 & 19:00-22:00, closed Wed, closed Nov-Feb, Piazza del Popolo 7, tel. 0187-808-107).

Ristorante Moresco serves large portions of pasta and seafood at reasonable prices in a vaulted, candlelit room decorated with Moorish-style frescoes. The best value is their €25 four-course tasting *menu* (doesn't include drinks, 2-person minimum). Skip the house white wine and order something more drinkable from their wine list (daily 12:00-14:00 & 19:00-21:00, until 23:00 in summer, may close Sun evenings in winter, reservations appreciated, Via Jacopo 24, tel. 0187-807-253, busy Roberto and Francesca).

Taverna Garibaldi is a good-value, cozy place on the most characteristic street in Levanto, serving focaccia with various toppings, made-to-order *farinata* (savory chickpea crêpe), 34 types of pizza, and salads (€8 light meals, daily in summer 19:30-22:00, closed Tue Sept-June, Via Garibaldi 57, tel. 0187-808-098).

La Picea serves up wood-fired pizzas to go, or dine at one of their few small tables (Tue-Sun 16:30-21:45, closed Mon, just off the corner near Via Varego at Via della Concia 18, tel. 0187-802-063).

A Picnic or Bite on the Go: Focaccerie, rosticcerie, and delis with take-out pasta abound on Via Dante Alighieri. **Focacceria il Falcone** has a great selection of focaccia with different toppings (daily 9:30-22:00, until 20:00 Oct-May, Via Cairoli 19, tel. 0187-807-370). For more picnic options, try the *mercato* (mornings except Sun It's fun to grab a crusty loaf of bread, then pair it with a pot of freshly made Genovese *pesto* from **Il Laboratorio del Pesto** (sometimes closed Wed afternoons, Via Dante 14, tel. 0187-807-441). The **Dimarket supermarket** just below the train station has a good deli counter and opens at 7:00—handy for those taking an early train. There are two **Crai supermarkets:** One is just off Via Jacopo da Levanto at Via del Municipio 5 (Mon-Sat 8:00-13:00 & 17:00-20:00, Sun 8:00-13:00 & 16:30-19:30); the other is nearby on Piazza Staglieno (for a shaded setting, lay out your spread on a bench in the grassy park at this piazza). Another excellent picnic spot is Piazza Cristoforo Colombo, located east of the swimming pool, with benches and sea views.

And for Dessert: Compare **Il Pinguino Gelateria** at Piazza Staglieno 2 (daily until late) with **Il Porticciolo Gelateria,** at the end of Via Cairoli at Piazzetta Marina (daily in summer, closed Mon Sept-June, mobile 393-228-1570).

Levanto Connections

From Levanto: To get to the Cinque Terre, take the **train** (2-3/hour, 4 minutes to Monterosso) or the **boat,** which stops at every Cinque Terre town—except Corniglia—before heading to Portovenere (2/day Easter-Oct, none Nov-Easter; €6 one-way to Monterosso, €11 round-trip, or €18 for half-day pass to Portovenere and scenic ride—departing Levanto at about 10:10 and 14:30, with 1-hour stop before return to Levanto; as much as €25 for all-day pass on a weekend to Portovenere; 1 return boat each day from Portovenere departs at about 17:00; pick up boat schedule and price sheet from TI or boat dock, or call 0187-732-987, or—on weekends—0187-777-727).

Sestri Levante

This peninsular town is squeezed as skinny as a hot dog between its two beaches. The pedestrian-friendly Corso Colombo, which runs down the middle of the peninsula, is lined with shops that sell take-away pizza, pastries, and beach paraphernalia.

Hans Christian Andersen enjoyed his visit here in the mid-1800s, writing, "What a fabulous evening I spent in Sestri Levante!" One of the bays—Baia delle Favole—is named in his honor (*favole* means "fairy tale"). The small mermaid curled on the edge of the fountain behind the TI is another nod to the beloved Danish storyteller.

During the last week of May, the town holds a street festival, culminating in a ceremony for locals who write the best fairy tales (four prizes for four age groups, from pre-kindergarten to adult). The "Oscar" awards are little mermaids.

Orientation to Sestri Levante

Tourist Information

From the train station, it's a five-minute walk to the TI, where you can pick up a map (Tue-Sun 9:30-13:00 & 14:00-17:30, closed Mon; go straight out of station on Via Roma, turn left at fountain in park, TI in next square—Piazza Sant'Antonio 10; tel. 0185-457-011).

Helpful Hints

Market Day: It's on Saturday at Piazza Aldo Moro (8:00-13:00).
Baggage Storage: None is available at the station.

Sights in Sestri Levante

Stroll the Town—From the TI, take Corso Colombo (to the left of Bermuda Bar, eventually turns into Via XXV Aprile), which runs up the peninsula. Follow this street—lively with shops, eateries, and delightful pastel facades—for about five minutes. Just before you get to the large white church at the end, turn off for either beach (free Silenzio beach is on your left). Or take the street on the left of the church to head uphill. You'll pass the evocative arches of a ruined chapel (bombed during World War II, and left as a memorial). Continue a few minutes farther, past a stony Romanesque church, to the Hotel Castelli and consider a drink at their view café (so-so view, reasonably priced drinks, daily 10:00-24:00, café entrance is at end of parking lot). The rocky, forested bluff at the end of the town's peninsula is actually the huge private backyard of this fancy hotel.

Beaches—These are named after the bays *(baie)* that they border. The bigger beach, Baia delle Favole, is divided up much of the year (May-Sept) into sections that you must pay to enter. The fees, which can soar up to €30 per day in August (no hourly rate), generally include chairs, umbrellas, and fewer crowds. There are several small free sections: at the ends and in the middle (look for *libere* signs, and ask *"Gratis?"* to make sure that it's free). For less-expensive sections of beach (where you can rent less than the works), ask for *spiaggia libera attrezzata* (spee-AH-jah LEE-behr-ah ah-treh-ZAHT-tah). The usual beach-town activities are clustered along this *baia:* boat rentals, sailing lessons, and bocce courts—ask if you can get in on a game.

The town's other beach, Baia del Silenzio, is narrow, virtually all free, and packed, providing a good chance to see Italian families at play. There isn't much more to do here than unroll a beach towel and join in. At the far end of Baia del Silenzio (under Hotel Helvetia) is Citto Beach bar, which offers front-row seats of bay views (drinks daily June-Aug 10:00-24:00, May and Sept-Oct until 20:00, sandwiches and salads at lunchtime only, closed Nov-April, Gilberto).

Sleeping in Sestri Levante

(€1 = about $1.40, country code: 39)

Prices listed here are the maximum during the high season (July-Aug). Prices will be €10-20 less April-June and September-October, and soft the rest of the year. Some hotels are closed off-season, so call ahead.

$$$ Hotel Due Mari, located in an old Genoese palazzo with sprawling public spaces, has three stars, 65 fine rooms, and a rooftop terrace with a super view of both beaches. Ideally, reserve well in advance. The extra services and grand communal spaces are the draw (small Db-€110, bigger Db-€140-190 depending on view and type of room, half-pension in aristocratic restaurant required July-Aug-€35/person, closed mid-Oct-Dec, air-con, Wi-Fi, elevator, garden, outdoor and heated indoor seawater swimming pools, wet sauna, small gym, parking-€15/day, take Corso Colombo to the end, hotel is behind church in Piazza Matteotti—take either alleyway flanking church, Vico del Coro 18, tel. 0185-42695, fax 0185-42698, www.duemarihotel.it, info@duemarihotel.it).

$$$ Hotel Helvetia, overlooking Baia del Silenzio, is another three-star bet, with 21 bright rooms, a large sun terrace, and a peaceful garden atmosphere—but apathetic management (viewless Db-€170, Db with view/balcony-€220, closed Nov-March, air-con, elevator, swimming pool, off-site parking-€5-15/day with free shuttle, from Corso Colombo turn left on Via Palestro and angle left at the small square to Via Cappuccini 43, tel. 0185-41175, fax 0185-457-216, www.hotelhelvetia.it, helvetia@hotelhelvetia.it).

$$$ Hotel Celeste, a dream for beach-lovers, rests along the waterfront. Its 41 rooms are modern and plainly outfitted—you pay for the sea breeze (Db-€165, with view and balcony €15-25 more, optional half-pension, air-con, elevator, Internet access, deals on beach chairs, attached beachside bar, Lungomare G. Descalzo 14, tel. 0185-485-005, fax 0185-411-166, www.hotelceleste.com, info @hotelceleste.com, Franco).

$$$ Hotel Genova, run by the Bertoni family, is a ship-shape hotel with 27 shiny-clean, modern, and cheery rooms, sunny lounge, rooftop sundeck, free loaner bikes, and a good location just two blocks from Baia delle Favole (Sb-€75, Db-€125, superior Db-€140, Tb-€169, ask for quieter room in back, air-con, elevator, Internet access and Wi-Fi, parking-€4/day; from the train station, walk straight ahead, turn right at the T-intersection, and find the cream building ahead on the right, Viale Mazzini 126; tel. 0185-41057, fax 0185-455-739, www.hotelgenovasestrilevante.com, info@hotelgenovasestrilevante.com).

$$ Albergo Marina's friendly Magda and her brother Santo rent 23 bright, peaceful, and clean rooms done in sea-foam green. Though the hotel is located on a busy boulevard, all rooms are at the back facing a quiet courtyard and parking lots...and priced right (Db-€65-80, half-pension optional, air-con, elevator, self-service laundry, pool table; exit the train station and angle left down Via Eraldo, at Piazza Repubblica take an easy left onto Via Fasce and find the hotel ahead on the right, Via Fasce 100; tel. & fax 0185-487-332, www.marinahotel.it, marinahotel@marinahotel.it).

$$ Villa Jolanda is a homey, kid-friendly, basic *pensione* with 17 simple rooms, five with little balconies but no views, new bathrooms, and a garden courtyard/sun terrace—perfect for families on a budget...and the owner's cats (Db-€75-90, Qb-€100-120, 3-night minimum stay required with advance reservation, €6.50 breakfast isn't worth it but owner Mario's €23 home-cooked dinners are, free parking, located near Baia del Silenzio—take alley just to the right of the church on Piazza Matteotti, Via Pozzetto 15, tel. & fax 0185-41354, www.villaiolanda.com, info@villaiolanda.com).

Eating in Sestri Levante

Everything I've listed is on classic Via XXV Aprile, which also abounds with *focaccerie*, take-out pizza by the slice, and little grocery shops. Assemble a picnic or try one of the places below.

At **L'Osteria Mattana,** where everyone shares long tables in two dining rooms (the second one is in the back, past the wood oven and brazier), you can mix with locals while enjoying traditional cuisine, listed on the chalkboard menus (Tue-Fri 19:30-22:00, Sat-Sun 12:30-14:30 & 19:30-22:30, closed Mon except in Aug, cash only; follow Corso Colombo from TI as it turns into Via XXV Aprile, restaurant on right at #36; tel. 0185-457-633, Marco).

Polpo Mario is classier but affordable, with a fun people-watching location on the main drag (€40 fixed-price tasting menu, Tue-Sun 12:15-15:00 & 19:30-23:00, closed Mon, Via XXV Aprile 163, tel. 0185-480-203).

Ristorante Mainolla offers pizzas, big salads, focaccia sandwiches, and reasonably priced pastas near Baia del Silenzio (daily in summer 12:00-16:00 & 19:00-22:00, closed Tue off-season, Via XXV Aprile 187, mobile 338-157-0877).

Gelato: Locals flock to **Ice Cream's Angels** at the intersection of Via XXV Aprile and Via della Chiusa. Riccardo and Elena artfully load up your cone with intermingling flavors, and top it with a dollop of Nutella chocolate-hazelnut cream (open daily until late in summer, closed Tue off-season, mobile 348-402-1604). **Bacciolo** enjoys a similar popularity among residents (closed Thu, Via XXV Aprile 51, on the right just before the church).

Supermarket: You can stock up on picnic supplies at two locations of **Carrefour Express** on Piazza della Repubblica, at #1 and #28 (daily 8:00-13:30 & 15:30-20:00).

Deli: For a take-out meal, head to **Rosticceria Bertolone** for roasted anything—beef, pork, chicken, or vegetables. Assemble an entire meal from their deli and ask them to heat it for you (Mon-Sat 7:30-13:00 & 16:00-19:30, closed Wed afternoon and all day Sun, Via Fasce 12, tel. 0185-487-098).

Sestri Levante Connections

Sestri Levante is just 20-40 minutes away from Monterosso by **train** (hourly connections with Monterosso, nearly hourly with other Cinque Terre towns).

Boats depart to the Cinque Terre, Santa Margherita Ligure, Portofino, and San Fruttuoso from the dock *(molo)* on the peninsula (boats run Easter-Oct; to get to the dock: facing the church in Piazza Matteotti, take the road on the right with the sea on your right, about halfway down Via P. Queirolo; tel. 0185-284-670, mobile 336-253-336, www.traghettiportofino.it).

Santa Margherita Ligure

If you need the movie stars' Riviera, park your yacht at Portofino. Or you can settle down in the nearby and more personable Santa

Margherita Ligure (15 minutes by bus from Portofino and one hour by train from the Cinque Terre). While Portofino's velour allure is tarnished by snobby residents and a nonstop traffic jam in peak season, Santa Margherita tumbles easily downhill from its train station. The town has a fun resort character and a breezy harborfront.

On a quick day trip from Milan or the Cinque Terre, walk the beach promenade and see the small old town of Santa Margherita Ligure before catching the bus (or boat) to Portofino to see what

all the fuss is about. With more time, Santa Margherita makes a fine overnight stop.

Orientation to Santa Margherita Ligure

Tourist Information

Pick up a map at the harborside TI on Piazza Veneto (daily April-Sept 9:30-12:30 & 14:30-19:00, Oct-March closes at 17:30 and all day Sun, tel. 0185-287-485, www.turismoinliguria.it).

Arrival by Train

To get from the station to the city center, take the stairs marked *Mare* (sea) down to the harbor. The harborfront promenade is as wide as the skimpy beach. (The real beaches, which are pebbly, are a 10-minute walk further on, past the port.)

To reach the pedestrian-friendly old town and the TI, take a right at Piazza Veneto (with the roundabout, flags, and park) onto Largo Antonio Giusti. For the TI, angle left on Via XXV Aprile. For the old town (a block off Piazza Veneto), head toward the TI, but turn left on Via Torino, which opens almost immediately onto Piazza Caprera, a square with a church and morning fruit vendors in the midst of pedestrian streets.

Helpful Hints

Internet Access: There are two terminals at **Papiluc Bar** (€3/30 minutes, daily 6:30 until late, Via del Arco 20, tel. 0185-282-580).

Post Office: It's just down the road from the train station on Via Roma (Mon-Fri 8:00-18:30, Sat 8:00-13:00, closed Sun, Via Roma 36).

Baggage Storage: There's no official left-luggage office, but day-trippers arriving by train may be able to stash their bags at the station's café-bar (outside the station on the left).

Bike Rental: GM Rent is at Via XXV Aprile 11 (€10/5 hours, €20/24 hours, also rents scooters and Smart Cars, daily 10:00-13:00 & 16:30-20:00, mobile 329-406-6274, www.gmrent.it, Francesco).

Taxi: Taxis wait outside the train station, and charge a minimum of €13 for a ride from the train station to anywhere in town (they justify the high price by the short tourist season).

Driver: Helpful taxi driver **Alessandro** is also available for airport transfers and local excursions (mobile 338-860-2349, www.alessandrotaxi.com, alessandrotaxi@yahoo.it).

Parking: The recommended **Hotel Mediterraneo** and **Villa Anita** offer free parking to their guests, and a few hotels have limited

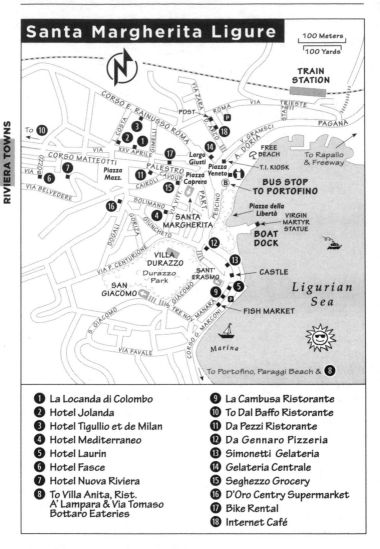

Santa Margherita Ligure

100 Meters
100 Yards

TRAIN STATION

To Rapallo & Freeway

FREE BEACH

T.I. KIOSK

BUS STOP TO PORTOFINO

Piazza della Libertà

VIRGIN MARTYR STATUE

BOAT DOCK

CASTLE

Ligurian Sea

FISH MARKET

SANTA MARGHERITA

VILLA DURAZZO
Durazzo Park

SAN GIACOMO

Marina

To Portofino, Paraggi Beach & ⑧

POST

CORSO E. RAINUSSO ROMA

CORSO MATTEOTTI

VIA BELVEDERE

Piazza Mazz.

PALESTRO

Largo Giusti

Piazza Veneto

Piazza Caprera

SANT' ERASMO

CORSO G. MARCONI

VIA FAVALE

- ❶ La Locanda di Colombo
- ❷ Hotel Jolanda
- ❸ Hotel Tigullio et de Milan
- ❹ Hotel Mediterraneo
- ❺ Hotel Laurin
- ❻ Hotel Fasce
- ❼ Hotel Nuova Riviera
- ❽ To Villa Anita, Rist. A' Lampara & Via Tomaso Bottaro Eateries
- ❾ La Cambusa Ristorante
- ❿ To Dal Baffo Ristorante
- ⑪ Da Pezzi Ristorante
- ⑫ Da Gennaro Pizzeria
- ⑬ Simonetti Gelateria
- ⑭ Gelateria Centrale
- ⑮ Seghezzo Grocery
- ⑯ D'Oro Centry Supermarket
- ⑰ Bike Rental
- ⑱ Internet Café

spots for a fee. When you reserve your room, mention that you'll have a car. Otherwise, try a private lot (about €10-15/half-day, €15-20/24 hours) such as **Autorimessa Europa,** next to the post office (Via Roma 38, tel. 0185-287-818). There's an hourly parking lot by the harbor, in front of the fish market (pay at blue machine in front of Laurin Hotel, Mon-Sat 8:00-20:00, Sun 8:00-23:00, first hour-€2, successive hours-€2.50). The TI has a list of parking spots (generally free where there are white lines) and paid parking lots.

Local Guide: Roberta De Beni knows the Ligurian Coast, its history, and its art very well (€100/half-day, €165/day, mobile 349-530-4778, www.xeniaguide.it, diodebe@inwind.it).

Self-Guided Walk

Welcome to Santa Margherita Ligure

Explore Santa Margherita Ligure on the following stroll.

• *Begin at Piazza della Libertà. Walk out to the tip of the boat dock and turn around to survey the...*

Town View: From here you can take in all of Santa Margherita Ligure, from the villas dotting the hills and the castle built in the 16th century (closed except for special exhibitions) to the exclusive hotels. Sharing the dock with you is a statue of "Santa Margherita Virgin Martyr."

• *Wander along the harborfront (down Corso Marconi) past the castle and to the...*

Marina: What's left of the town's fishing fleet ties up here. The fishing industry survives, drag-netting octopus, shrimp, and miscellaneous "blue fish"—plus mountains of anchovies attracted to midnight lamps. The fish market (inside the rust-colored building with arches and columns) wiggles weekdays at about, oh, maybe 16:00-20:00 or so. Residents complain that it's easier to buy their locally caught fresh fish in Milan than here.

• *Behind the fish market, up a flight of stairs by the war memorial, stands the...*

Oratory of Sant'Erasmo: This small church is named for St. Erasmus (a.k.a. "St. Elmo"), the protector of sailors. Notice the fine and typically local black-and-white pebble mosaic *(riseu)* in front of the church (with maritime themes). The church is actually an "oratory," where a brotherhood of faithful men who did anonymous good deeds congregated and worshipped. It's decorated with ships and paintings of storms that—thanks to St. Erasmus—the local seafarers survived. The huge crosses are carried through town on special religious holidays (the church is supposedly open only during Mass, but often open at other times, too).

• *Next, double back to climb the looooong stairway (Via Tre Novembre) overlooking the bay to reach the...*

Church of San Giacomo: Even though this is a secondary church in a secondary town, it's impressively lavish (daily 7:30-19:00, may close earlier in winter, avoid visiting during Mass—usually 7:45-9:00). The region's aristocrats amassed wealth from trade in the 11th to the 15th centuries. When Constantinople fell to the Turks, free trade in the Mediterranean stopped and Genovese traders became bankers—making even more money. A popular saying of the day was, "Silver is born in America, lives in Spain, and dies in Genoa." Bankers here served Spain's 17th-century

Rise of a Resort: The History of Santa Margherita Ligure

This town, like the entire region (from the border of France to La Spezia), was once ruled by the Republic of Genoa. In the 16th century, when Arab pirates from North Africa plagued the entire coastal area, Genoa built castles in the towns and lookout towers in the neighboring hills.

At the time, Santa Margherita was actually two bickering towns—each with its own bay. In 1800, Napoleon came along, took over the Republic of Genoa, and turned the rival towns into one city—naming it Porto Napoleone. When Napoleon fell in 1815, the town stayed united and took the name of the patron saint of its leading church, Santa Margherita.

In 1850, residents set to work creating a Riviera resort. They imported palm trees from North Africa and paved a fine beach promenade. Santa Margherita (and the surrounding area) was studded with fancy villas built by the aristocracy of Genoa (which was controlled by just 35 families). English, Russian, and German aristocrats also discovered the town in the 19th century. Mass tourism only hit in the last generation. Even with the increased crowds, the town decided to stay chic and kept huge developments out. Its neighbor, Rapallo, chose the extreme opposite—giving the Italian language a new word for uncontrolled growth ruining a once-cute town: *rapallizzazione*.

royalty and aristocracy, and the accrued wealth paid for a Golden Age of art. Wander the church, noticing the inlaid-marble floors and chapels.

• *Step out of the church and enjoy the sea view. Then turn left and step into...*

Durazzo Park (Parco Comunale Villa Durazzo): This park was an abandoned shambles until 1973, when the city took it over (free, daily May-Sept 9:00-19:00, maybe until 20:00 July-Aug, Oct-April 9:00-17:00). Today it's a delight, with a breezy café enjoyed mostly by locals (generally daily from 10:30 except closed Tue May-Aug) and free Wi-Fi (ask at the cafe for the password). The garden has two distinct parts: the carefully coiffed Italian garden (designed to complement the villa's architecture) and the calculatedly wild "English garden" below. The Italian garden is famous for its varied collection of palm trees, and an extensive collection of camellias. It's OK to feed the large turtles in the central pond (they like bits of fish or meat).

• *In the building next to the café, you'll see...*

Villa Durazzo: This was the home of a local journalist and writer, Vittorio G. Rossi (1898-1978), whose office has been preserved as he left it. Typical of the region, this palazzo has some period furniture, several grand pianos, chandeliers, and paintings strewn with cupids on the walls and ceilings. Look for King Umberto's letter offering condolences on Rossi's death. For most people, it's probably not worth the entry fee (€5.50, more for special exhibits; daily 9:00-13:00 & 14:00-18:00, Oct-March until 17:00, last entry 30 minutes before closing, WC opposite entry on left, tel. 0185-293-135, www.villadurazzo.it, villa.durazzo @comunesml.it). Classical music concerts are held here in July and August (ask at TI or villa ticket desk, or call for the schedule).

• *Your self-guided walk is over. Enjoy the park.*

Sights in Santa Margherita Ligure

Church of Santa Margherita (Basilica di Nostra Signora della Rosa)—The town's main church is textbook Italian Baroque. Its 18th-century facade hides a 17th-century interior. The chapels to the right of the high altar contain religious "floats" used in local festival parades. The wooden groups in the niches higher up used to be part of the processions, too. The altar is typical of 17th-century Ligurian altars—shaped like a boat, with lots of shelf space for candles, flowers, and relics. Remember, Baroque is like theater. After the Vatican II decrees of the 1960s, priests began to face their flocks instead of the old altars. For this reason, all over the Catholic world, modern tables serving as post-Vatican II altars stand in front of earlier altars that are no longer the center of attention during the Mass.

Cost and Hours: Free, daily 7:30-12:00 & 15:00-18:30, tel. 0185-286-555.

Via Palestro—This promenade (a.k.a. *caruggio*—"the big street" in local dialect) is *the* strolling street for window-shopping, people-watching, and studying the characteristic Art Nouveau house painting from about 1900. Before 1900, people distinguished their buildings with pastel paint and distinctive door and window frames. Then they decided to get fancy and paint entire exteriors with false balconies, weapons, saints, beautiful women, and 3-D Gothic concentrate.

As you wander from the Church of Santa Margherita inland, pop into the fanciest grocer-deli in town—the recommended

Seghezzo (immediately to the right of the church on Via Cavour). Locals know that this venerable institution has whatever odd ingredient the most obscure recipe calls for.

Farther up Via Palestro, you might drop into the traditional old **Panificio** bakery for a slice of fresh focaccia. Saying *"Vorrei un etto di focaccia"* will get you a Ligurian olive-oily, 100-gram, €1.50 hunk of every kid's favorite beach munchie. Locals claim the best focaccia in Italy is made along this coast.

Markets—On weekday afternoons, fishing boats unload their catch, which is then sold to waiting customers at **Mercato del Pesce** (roughly Mon-Fri 17:00-20:00, opens an hour earlier for wholesalers, Oct-April might open at 15:30). Find it in the rust-colored building with arches and columns on Corso Marconi, on the harbor, just past the castle. The open-air market, a commotion of clothes and produce, is held every Friday morning along Corso Matteotti, inland from Piazza Mazzini (8:00-13:00). Piazza Caprera (facing the main church) daily hosts a few farmers selling their produce from stalls.

Beaches—The handiest free Santa Margherita beaches are just below the train station toward the boat dock. But the best beaches are on the south side of town. Among these, I like "Gio and Rino beach" (just before Covo di Nord Est)—not too expensive, with fun, creative management and a young crowd. Also nice is the beach on the south side of Hotel Miramare, which offers a more relaxing sun-worshipping experience. Both beaches have free entry and rentable chairs and umbrellas. They're a 20-minute walk from downtown, or take the bus from either the train station or Piazza Veneto (€1.50 each way if bought in advance from kiosk, newsstands, tobacco shops, or the green ATP ticket office next to the TI; €3 if bought on board).

Paraggi beach, which is halfway to Portofino (with an easy bus connection—see "Portofino," later in this chapter), is better than any Santa Margherita beach, but it's *very* expensive. One Paraggi beach operator, Bosetti, offers a reasonable rate (€25/day, no hourly rates, includes umbrella, lounge chair, and towel), while rates at other beaches may soar up to €50 per day in July and August. In high season, the Paraggi beach may be all booked up by big shots from Portofino, which has no beach—only rocks. Off-season, the entire Paraggi beach is all yours and free of charge. A skinny patch of sand smack-dab in the middle of Paraggi beach is free year-round.

Sleeping in Santa Margherita Ligure

(€1 = about $1.40, country code: 39)

All of these are in the center. La Locanda di Colombo, Hotel Jolanda, and Hotel Tigullio et de Milan are closest to the station.

Prices listed here are the maximum price for the high season of July-August. Expect April-June and September-October to be €10-15 cheaper, and the rest of the year to be cheaper still.

$$$ La Locanda di Colombo has six stylish and contemporary rooms and two small, relaxing patios (Db-€150, tell them "Rick sent me" to get a 5 percent discount on stays of 1-3 days, 10 percent discount on longer stays; air-con, disabled access, Via XXV Aprile 12, tel. 0185-293-129, fax 0185-291-937, www.la locandadicolombo.it, sml@lalocandadicolombo.it, welcoming hosts Massimiliano and Raffaella).

$$$ Hotel Jolanda, just around the corner from La Locanda di Colombo, is a solid, professionally run hotel with 50 rooms, a revolving door, a good breakfast buffet, and a friendly staff. With lavish public spaces and regal colors, this place makes you feel like nobility (Db-€150, superior Db-€170, 10 percent discount with this book if you mention it when you reserve, Internet access and Wi-Fi, air-con, elevator, free one-hour use of small weight room, wet and dry saunas, Jacuzzi, 10 free loaner bikes on request, Via Luisito Costa 6, tel. 0185-287-512, fax 0185-284-763, www.hotel jolanda.it, info@hoteljolanda.it).

$$$ Hotel Tigullio et de Milan, run by Giuseppe of Hotel Jolanda, has equally fine rooms with creamy hues and lower prices. You don't get all the luxurious extras, but the breezy sun terrace on top—with a bar in summertime—makes for a relaxing retreat (Db-€140, bigger Db with terrace-€150, 10 percent discount with this book if you mention it when you reserve, air-con, elevator but lots of stairs down to reception, parking-€20-25, Via Rainusso 6, tel. 0185-287-455, fax 0185-281-860, www.hoteltigullio.eu, info @hoteltigullio.eu).

$$$ Hotel Mediterraneo, run by the Melegatti family, offers 30 spacious rooms (a few with balconies or sun terraces) in a family-friendly, comfy 18th-century palazzo a five-minute walk from Piazza Veneto. They have a park-like sun garden with lounge chairs and lots of semi-private space. Pia Pauli makes great Ligurian specialties for dinner (Sb-€100, Db-€150, Tb-€160, great breakfast, five-course dinner-€30/person, free laundry service with 3-day stay or longer, free parking, free loaner bikes, closed Jan-March, take street immediately to the right of Church of Santa Margherita and find hotel straight ahead at Via della Vittoria 18A, tel. 0185-286-881, fax 0185-286-882, www.sml-mediterraneo.it, info@sml-mediterraneo.it).

$$$ Hotel Laurin offers slick, modern, air-conditioned, American-style lodgings fixated on harborfront views. All of its 43 rooms face the sea, most have terraces, and there's a small pool on the sundeck, as well as a gym and wet sauna. As it's a Best Western, it feels corporate (Sb-€157, Db-€222, 10 percent discount if you book direct—mention this book when you reserve and show book on arrival, double-paned windows, elevator, 15-yard walk past the castle or €15 taxi ride from station, Corso Marconi 3, tel. 0185-289-971, fax 0185-285-709, www.laurinhotel.it, info@laurin hotel.it).

$$$ **Hotel Fasce,** a 16-room hotel surrounded by flowers and greenery, is run enthusiastically by intense Englishwoman Jane Fasce, her husband Aristide, and son Alessandro. Jane gets mixed reviews from my readers—some find her helpful, while others find her rules too strict...my advice is to toe the line (Sb-€100, Db-€124, Tb-€145, Qb-€190, see website for deals, no-nonsense 21-day cancellation policy, two rooms have private bathroom located across the hall, no elevator, free loaner bikes, rooftop garden, laundry service-€18, parking-€20, free round-trip train tickets to Cinque Terre with 3-night stay if you book room direct or through their website, 10-minute walk or €15 cab ride from station at Via Bozzo 3, tel. 0185-286-435, fax 0185-283-580, www.hotelfasce.it, hotel fasce@hotelfasce.it).

$$$ **Villa Anita** is an elegant-yet-homey family hotel run by hospitable Daniela and her friendly son, Sandro. They rent 12 tidy rooms—nearly all with terraces, and several with new, high-tech bathrooms—overlooking a peaceful residential neighborhood just a five-minute walk from the seaside boulevard. Daniela makes great cakes, and the in-house chef offers a varying menu of Ligurian specialties (Db-€140, optional half-pension-€90, air-con, free Wi-Fi, free parking, €15 cab ride from station, Via Tigullio 10, tel. 0185-286-543, fax 0185-283-005, www.hotelvillaanita.com, info@hotelvillaanita.com).

$$$ **Hotel Nuova Riviera** is an old villa surrounded by a garden, with nine institutional-feeling rooms (Db-€115, Tb-€138, Qb-€165, these prices good in 2012 if you book direct and mention this book when you reserve, additional 5 percent discount with cash, fans, some balconies, no elevator, 15-minute walk from station or easy cab ride; if you're driving, follow signs to hospital, then watch for hotel signs on Piazza Mazzini; if you're walking, enter Piazza Mazzini and see signs from there; Via Belvedere 10, tel. & fax 0185-287-403, www.nuovariviera.com, info@nuova riviera.com). They also run a nearby annex with six renovated rooms and one apartment with a tiny corner kitchen (Db-€100, Tb-€110, Qb-€125, cash only, breakfast at Hotel Nuova Riviera is optional and extra, tel. 0185-287-403, www.sabinirentals.com, sabinirentals@gmail.com).

Eating in Santa Margherita Ligure

Ristorante "A' Lampara" is the locals' favorite for *casalinga* (home-style) Genovese cuisine, prepared by the endearing Barbieri family: Mamma Maria Luisa oversees the dining room, son Mario cooks, and daughter Natalina serves. Try their specialties, such as *ravioli di pesce* (homemade fish ravioli with red mullet sauce) or *pansotti con salsa di noci*—cheese ravioli with walnut sauce (Fri-Wed 12:30-14:00 & 19:30-22:00, closed Thu, veggie options; follow Corso Marconi 4 blocks past the fish market, turn right onto Via Maragliano, and find #33 a block and a half ahead on left; tel. 0185-288-926).

La Cambusa is perched above the culinary heart of Santa Margherita Ligure—the fish market. Popular with tourists and resident romantics, its terrace has an unbeatable view over the harbor. In cooler weather, the terrace is covered and heated. Pick your favorite yacht while tucking into their seafood dishes with a Ligurian twist (€13 pasta, €20 main dishes, July-Sept daily 9:00-15:00 & 19:00-24:00 except closed Thu morning, Oct-June closed all day Thu, Via T. Bottaro, tel. 0185-287-410; Luciano, wife Antonella, and serious but efficient Vittorio).

Dal Baffo is a bustling mom-and-pop eatery popular for its traditional Ligurian specialties, including homemade pasta, wood-fired pizzas (folks queue up to watch the *pizzaioli* make their €7 pies to go), fresh fish, and grilled steaks at reasonable prices (Wed-Mon 12:00-15:00 & 19:00-23:30, closed Tue; from Piazza Caprera, head inland—both pedestrian streets eventually turn into busy Corso Matteotti; Corso Matteotti 56, tel. 0185-288-987).

Da Pezzi, with a cheap cafeteria-style atmosphere, is packed with locals at midday and at night. They're munching *farinata* (crêpes made from chickpeas, available Oct-May) standing at the bar, or enjoying pesto and fresh fish in the dining room. Consider the deli counter with its Genovese picnic ingredients (Sun-Fri 12:00-14:00 & 18:15-21:00, closed Sat, Via Cavour 21, tel. 0185-285-303, Giancarlo and Giobatta).

Waterfront Dining: All along Via Tomaso Bottaro, you'll find restaurants, pizzerias, and bars serving food with a harbor view. **Da Gennaro Pizzeria,** at Piazza della Libertà 30 by the boat dock, makes popular Neapolitan-style pizzas. **Bar Giuli,** the only place actually on the harbor, serves forgettable salads and sandwiches for a reasonable price (about 150 yards south of the fish market).

Gelato: The best *gelateria* I found in town—with chocolate-truffle *tartufato*—is **Simonetti** (daily 8:30 until late, closed Mon off-season, under the castle, closest to the water at Piazza della Libertà 48). **Gelateria Centrale,** just off Piazza Veneto near the cinema, serves up their specialty—*pinguino* (penguin), a cone with your choice of gelato dipped in chocolate (daily 7:00-late, closed Wed Sept-May).

Groceries: **Seghezzo** is classiest and great for a meal to go—ask them to *riscaldare* (heat up) their white *lasagne al pesto* or grilled veggies (daily June-Aug 7:30-13:00 & 15:30-20:00, closed Wed Sept-May, right of the church on Via Cavour). The **D'Oro Centry** supermarket, just off Piazza Mazzini at #38, has better prices (Mon-Sat 8:00-13:30 & 15:30-19:30, Sun 8:00-13:00, during summer Sat open all day long, tel. 0185-286-470).

Santa Margherita Ligure Connections

From Santa Margherita Ligure by Train to: Sestri Levante (2/hour, 30 minutes, €2.40), **Monterosso** (at least hourly, 45 minutes, €4.10), **La Spezia** (hourly, 1-1.5 hours, €5.50), **Pisa** (1-2/hour, 2-2.5 hours, InterCity/IC goes direct, other connections may require transfer in La Spezia, €14.50), **Milan** (8/day, 2-2.5 hours, more with transfer in Genoa, €19), **Ventimiglia**/French border (4/day, 4 hours; or hourly with change in Genoa, €13), **Venice** (8/day, 6-7 hours with 1-3 changes, €41-50). For **Florence,** transfer in Pisa (8/day, 3.5-4 hours, €20-26).

By Boat to the Cinque Terre: For the latest, pick up a schedule of departures and excursion options from the TI, ask at your hotel, call 0185-284-670 or 335-709-0870, or check online at www.traghettiportofino.it. The routes mentioned below run at least twice weekly from May through September or October, increasing in frequency in July and August.

The "Linea 3" boat does an all-day trip that includes two stopovers: one hour in Vernazza and three hours in Portovenere, plus a scenic trip around an island (May-mid-Oct depart Sun at 9:00, plus Tue and Thu late July-mid-Sept, €21 one-way, €32 round-trip).

The half-day "Linea 4" boat sails to the Cinque Terre with a one-hour stopover in Vernazza (May-Oct depart Mon and Fri at 13:30, €17 one-way, €24.50 round-trip).

The "Super Cinque Terre, Linea 5" boat offers day-trip cruises from Santa Margherita Ligure to the Cinque Terre, departing at 8:45 and stopping in three Cinque Terre towns: three hours in Monterosso, and an hour each in Vernazza and Riomaggiore (May-Sept Wed and Sat only, €21 one-way, €32 round-trip).

Portofino

Santa Margherita Ligure, with its aristocratic architecture, hints at old money, whereas nearby Portofino, with its sleek shops, reeks

of new money. Fortunately, a few pizzerias, *focaccerie,* bars, and grocery shops are mixed in with Portofino's jewelry shops, art galleries, and haute couture boutiques, making the town affordable. The *piccolo* harbor, classic Italian architecture, and wooded peninsula can even turn glitzy Portofino into an appealing package. It makes a fun day trip from Santa Margherita Ligure.

Ever since the Romans founded Portofino for its safe harbor, it has had a strategic value (appreciated by everyone from Napoleon to the Nazis). In the 1950s, *National Geographic* did a beautiful exposé on the idyllic port, and locals claim that's when the Hollywood elite took note. Liz Taylor and Richard Burton came here annually (as did Liz Taylor and Eddie Fisher). During one famous party, Rex Harrison dropped his Oscar into the bay (it was recovered). Ava Gardner came down from her villa each evening for a drink—sporting her famous fur coat. Greta Garbo loved to swim naked in the harbor, not knowing that half the town was watching. Truman Capote also called Portofino home. But VIPs were also here a century earlier. In one of his books, Friedrich Nietzsche wrote about philosophizing with the mythical prophet Zarathustra on the path between Portofino and Santa Margherita.

My favorite Portofino plan: Visit for the evening. Leave Santa Margherita on the bus at about 16:30 and hike the last 20 minutes from Paraggi beach. Explore Portofino. Splurge for a drink on the harborfront, or get a take-out fruity sundae (*paciugo*; pah-CHOO-goh) and sit by the water. Then return by bus to Santa Margherita for dinner (confirm late departures). Portofino does offer fancy harborside dining, but the quality doesn't match the high prices.

Getting to Portofino

Portofino makes an easy day trip from Santa Margherita by bus, boat, bike, or foot.

By Bus: Catch bus #82 from Santa Margherita's train station or at bus stops along the harbor (main stop in front of TI, €1, 2-3/hour, 15 minutes, goes to Paraggi or Portofino). Buy tickets at the bar next to the station, at Piazza Veneto's green bus kiosk (next door to the TI; daily 7:15-19:45), from the green machine on

RIVIERA TOWNS

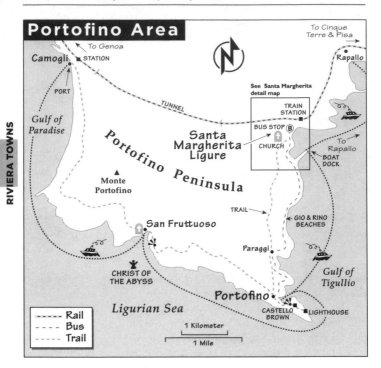

Portofino Area

To Genoa

To Cinque Terre & Pisa

Camogli STATION

Rapallo

PORT

TUNNEL

See Santa Margherita detail map

TRAIN STATION

BUS STOP B

CHURCH

Gulf of Paradise

Santa Margherita Ligure

Portofino Peninsula

To Rapallo

BOAT DOCK

Monte Portofino

San Fruttuoso

TRAIL

GIO & RINO BEACHES

Paraggi

CHRIST OF THE ABYSS

Gulf of Tigullio

Portofino

Ligurian Sea

CASTELLO BROWN

LIGHTHOUSE

- - - - - Rail
- - - - Bus
- - - - Trail

1 Kilometer

1 Mile

the side of the kiosk, or at any newsstand, tobacco shop, or shop that displays a *Biglietti Bus* sign. You can usually buy tickets on the bus—for double the cost. If you're at the Piazza Veneto kiosk, grab a bus schedule, which will come in handy if you travel in the evening (last bus around 23:00, #882).

In Portofino, get tickets at the newsstand or from the machine next to the bus stop (go uphill and you'll come to Piazza Martiri della Libertà, machine and bus stop on right side, directions in English).

By Boat: The boat makes the 15-minute trip with more class and without the traffic jams (€5.50 one-way, €8.50 round-trip, €0.50 more on Sun and holidays; daily May-Sept nearly hourly departures 10:15-16:15, Oct-April at 10:15 and 14:15 only; dock is a 2-minute walk from Piazza Veneto off Piazza Martiri della Libertà, call to confirm or pick up schedule from TI or your hotel, tel. 0185-284-670, mobile 336-253-336, check at www.traghetti portofino.it). This company also runs boats from Santa Margherita to the Cinque Terre. The boat from Portofino back to Santa Margherita departs nearly hourly in summer (May-Sept daily 12:00-18:00; Oct-April at 12:00 and 16:00 only).

The boats run between Rapallo and the San Fruttuoso Abbey, stopping en route at Santa Margherita Ligure and Portofino.

(Another boat line runs from Recco, Camogli, and Punta Chiappa to the abbey.)

By Bike: The 25-minute bike ride from Santa Margherita to Portofino is doable for cautious cyclists. While there are no steep hills to struggle up, the road is narrow, with many blind corners. Many of my recommended hotels provide free loaner bikes (though they may not be in the best condition); you can also rent your own wheels.

On Foot: To hike the entire distance from Santa Margherita Ligure to Portofino, you have two options: You can follow the sidewalk along (and sometimes hanging over) the sea (1 hour, 2.5 miles)—although traffic can be noisy. Or, if you're hardy and ambitious, you can take a quieter two-hour hike by leaving Santa Margherita at Via Maragliano, then follow the Ligurian-symbol trail markers (look for red-and-white stripes—they're not always obvious, sometimes numbered according to the path you're on, usually painted on rocks or walls, especially at junctions). This hike takes you high into the hills. Keep left after Cappelletta delle Gave. Several blocks past a castle, you'll drop down into the Paraggi beach, where you'll take the Portofino trail the rest of the way.

Bus and Hike Option: For a shorter hike (20 minutes) into Portofino, ride bus #82 from Santa Margherita only as far as the small but ritzy Paraggi beach. (Ask on board where to get off, as the Paraggi stop is not labeled—watch for an inland bay with green water and a sandy beach.) At the far end of the beach, cross the street, climb the steps, and follow the hilly, paved trail marked *Pedonali per Portofino* high above the road. Twenty minutes later, you'll enter Portofino at a yellow-and-gray-striped church labeled *Divo Martino*—which I figure means "the divine Martin" and has something to do with Dean Martin giving us all "Volare" (which I couldn't get out of my head for the rest of the day).

Orientation to Portofino

Tourist Information

Portofino's TI is downhill from the bus stop, on your right under the portico. Pick up a free town map and a rudimentary hiking map (Easter-Sept daily 10:00-13:00 & 14:00-18:00; Oct-Easter Tue-Sat 9:30-13:30 & 14:00-17:00, closed Sun-Mon; Via Roma 35, tel. 0185-269-024).

Sights in Portofino

Museo del Parco—For an artsy break, walk around the harbor to the right, where you can stroll around a park littered with 148 contemporary sculptures by top artists (€5, May-Oct Wed-Mon

10:00-13:00 & 15:00-19:00, closed Tue, closed Nov-April and in bad weather, mobile 337-333-737).

Hikes—One option is the paved stone path that winds up and down to the **lighthouse** *(faro)* at a scenic point with a bar (bar open May-Sept, hedges block views until the end, 25-minute walk). Consider popping into **Castello Brown,** a medieval castle, on the way. It features lush gardens and a black-and-white portrait gallery of stars and famous personages who once frequented Portofino, including Clark Gable, Sophia Loren, Kim Novak, Grace Kelly, John Wayne, Ernest Hemingway, Humphrey Bogart, and Lauren Bacall. Original decorations and photos are explained in English (€4, daily 10:00-19:00, until 17:00 in winter, tel. 0185-267-101, www.castellobrown.it).

Or you could stroll the hilly pedestrian promenade through the trees from Portofino to **Paraggi beach,** and, if you're lucky, see a wild boar en route (20 minutes, path starts to the right of yellow-and-gray-striped Divo Martino church—look for clock tower, parallels main road, ends at ritzy Paraggi beach, where it's easy to catch bus back to Santa Margherita Ligure).

Another option is to hike out to **San Fruttuoso Abbey** and the nearby underwater Christ statue (described next; the hike there is steep at beginning and end, takes about 2.5 hours from Portofino—pick up the trailhead at the inland-most point of town, past Piazza della Libertà and the *carabinieri* station; you can also hike all the way there from Santa Margherita in about 4.5 hours via Portofino).

Near Portofino

San Fruttuoso Abbey—This 11th-century abbey is accessible only by foot (a 2.5-hour hike from Portofino, 4.5 hours from Santa Margherita) or boat (from either Portofino or Santa Margherita; abbey entry-€5, more for special exhibits; June-Sept daily 10:00-17:45; Oct-May daily 10:00-15:45 except closed Mon in winter; last entry 45 minutes before closing, tel. 0185-772-703). But the abbey itself isn't the main attraction. The more intriguing draw is 60 feet underwater, offshore from the abbey: the statue *Christ of the Abyss (Cristo degli Abissi).* A rowboat will take you from the dock below the Portofino boat dock to the statue, where you can look down through a lens to just barely see the arms of Jesus—outstretched,  reaching upward. Some people bring goggles and dive in for a better view. The statue was placed there in 1954 for the divine protection of the region's divers. As the rowboats don't run in rough seas, call the abbey to confirm before making the trip (about €4, 20-minute round-trip, rowboats run only during boat arrival hours from Portofino—generally daily May-Sept 9:00-17:00).

From Easter through September, boats continue north from San Fruttuoso Abbey to Punta Chiappa and Camogli (€5 one-way, can return to Santa Margherita by train or buy round-trip boat tickets, call 0185-772-091 or inquire at Portofino or Santa Margherita TI for information).

Eating in Portofino

Food and drink are expensive in Portofino. **Bar Moreno da Ucio,** on the first outdoor terrace along the harbor to the left of the TI, has somewhat reasonable drink prices...by Portofino standards (€8 sparkling wine, €3 cappuccino, Fri-Wed 7:30-late, closed Thu).

South of the Cinque Terre

La Spezia

While just a quick train ride away from the fanciful Cinque Terre (20-30 minutes), the working town of La Spezia feels like "reality Italy." Primarily a jumping-off point for travelers, the town is slim on sights, and has no beaches.

The pedestrian zone on Via del Prione to the gardens along the harbor makes a pleasant stroll. The nearly deserted **Museo Amedeo Lia** displays Italian paintings from the 13th to 18th centuries, including minor works by Venetian masters Titian, Tintoretto, and Canaletto (€6.50, Tue-Sun 10:00-18:00, closed Mon, last entry 30 minutes before closing, English descriptions on laminated sheets in most rooms, audioguide-€3, WCs down the hall from ticket desk, no photos allowed, 10-minute walk from station at Via del Prione 234, tel. 0187-731-100, http://mal.spezia net.it).

Stay in the Cinque Terre if you can. But if you're in a bind, I've listed several La Spezia accommodations. I've also listed (under "Eating in La Spezia") some places to grab a meal while you wait for a train.

Orientation to La Spezia

Tourist Information

The TI is in a separate building in front of the north end of the train station, by the pine trees (daily April-Sept 9:00-19:00,

Oct-March 9:00-17:00, tel. 0187-770-900, www.turismoprovincia
.laspezia.it). The Cinque Terre National Park office is inside the
train station (daily 7:00-13:00 & 13:30-20:00, until 17:00 off-
season, www.parconazionale5terre.it). A second TI is near the
waterfront (with same phone and hours as the train station TI,
Viale Italia 5).

Arrival in La Spezia

By Train: Get off at the La Spezia Centrale stop. You can check
your bags at the train station (see "Helpful Hints," below). Exit
the station down the road to the left, where several recommended hotels and eateries are located. From beside the TI, a less-
convenient set of stairs descends to Via Fiume. A new train station
exit may be added when work on the underground parking lot is
complete.

By Car: A parking lot is being built underneath the train station, but may not be finished by your visit. You'll find free parking
at Piazza d'Armi; from there, it's a 20-minute walk to the train
station, or take the €1 shuttle service to Piazza Brin, a five-minute

Legend:
1. Hotel Firenze e Continentale
2. Hotel Astoria
3. Hotel Venezia
4. Albergo Parma
5. La Stazione del Golfo dei Poeti Rooms
6. La Stazione del Golfo dei Poeti Reception
7. Casa da Nè/ Tre Frè Rooms
8. L'Arca di Noè B&B
9. Ristorante Roma da Marcellin
10. Il Pomodoro Pizzeria
11. Covered Market
12. Supermarket & Launderette
13. Piazza d'Armi (Free Parking)
14. Piazza d'Armi Shuttle Drop-Off
15. AciPark Garage
16. Portovenere Bus Stop

RIVIERA TOWNS

walk from the station (3/hour). To reach Piazza d'Armi from the highway, follow the La Spezia autostrada as it becomes Viale Carducci and ends at Viale Italia, then turn left and follow the road as it bends right, following signs for parking.

A guarded parking garage is on Via Crispi, just after the Galleria (tunnel) Spallanzani on the right. Look for the *AciPark* sign (€20/day for 1-3 days, €16/day for longer stays, Mon-Fri 7:00-20:15, Sat 7:00-13:30, closed Sun, reserve in advance only if you'll be arriving when they're closed, tel. 0187-510-545, aci park@libero.it).

Helpful Hints

Market Days: A colorful covered market sets up in Piazza Cavour (Mon-Sat 8:00-13:00). On Fridays, a huge all-day open-air market sprawls along Viale Garibaldi, about six blocks from the station.

Baggage Storage: A left-luggage service is at the train station along track 1 (facing the tracks on platform 1, go left; it's next to the WC). It's secure, though it isn't always staffed—ring the bell to the left of the doorway to call the attendant. Since you may have to wait, allow plenty of time to pick up your baggage before departing (€3/12 hours, daily 8:00-22:00, they'll photocopy your passport).

Laundry: A handy self-service launderette is just below the train station. Head down toward town, and immediately at the first piazza take a sharp right on Via Fiume—it's on your left at #95 (€8.50 one-hour wash and dry, Mon-Sat 8:00-22:00, Sun 9:00-22:00, mobile 348-543-7924, Edoardo).

Supermarket: DiMeglio is at Via Fiume 125, near the recommended launderette (daily 8:00-20:00, tel. 0187-704-059).

Booking Agency: Cinque Terre Riviera books rooms and apartments in La Spezia, the Cinque Terre, and Portovenere for a 10 percent markup (Mon-Fri 9:30-13:00 & 15:00-19:30, closed Sat-Sun, check website for day trips and cooking lessons, Via Picedi 18, tel. 0187-520-702, www.cinqueterreriviera.com, info@cinqueterreriviera.com).

Getting to the Cinque Terre: Trains leave at least twice hourly for the Cinque Terre, though not all trains stop at all towns. The Cinque Terre Treno Park Card (covers train ride to Cinque Terre as well as hiking fee) is sold at the train-station ticket window and at the national park office in the station (see "Tourist Information," at the beginning of this section).

Sleeping in La Spezia

(€1 = about $1.40, country code: 39)
Remember, sleep in La Spezia only as a last resort. These hotels and rooms are within a five-minute walk of La Spezia's station—except the last two listings, which are for drivers only.

Hotels

$$$ Hotel Firenze e Continentale is grand and Old World, but newly restored with a mountain-view breakfast room to boot. Just to the left of the station, its 67 rooms have all the usual comforts. Maria Gabriella will throw in a Cinque Terre food specialty for my readers (Sb-€85, Db-€125, large superior Db-€150, these special prices when you book direct with this book, cheaper during slow times, non-smoking rooms, double-paned windows, air-con, elevator, outdoor parking-€8/day, indoor parking-€18/day, Via Paleocapa 7, tel. 0187-713-200, fax 0187-714-930, www.hotel firenzecontinentale.it, info@hotelfirenzecontinentale.it).

$$ Hotel Astoria, with 48 decent rooms, has a combination lobby and breakfast room as large as a school cafeteria. It's a fine backup if the hotels nearer the train station are full (Db without air-con-€80; Db-€130 for the 10 summery, modern rooms with air-con and double-paned windows; elevator, free parking garage; take Via Milano left of Albergo Parma, go 3 blocks, and turn left to reach Via Roma 139; tel. 0187-714-655, fax 0187-714-425, www .albergoastoria.com, info@albergoastoria.com).

$$ Hotel Venezia, across the street from Hotel Firenze e Continentale, is run with low energy but its 19 rooms are pleasantly modern and recently remodeled (Sb-€55, Db-€90, air-con, elevator, free parking out front but must request when you reserve, Via Paleocapa 10, tel. & fax 0187-733-465, www.hotelveneziala spezia.it, hotelvenezia@telematicaitalia.it).

$$ Albergo Parma, with 36 rooms, is a little worn around the edges but inexpensive (D-€50, Db-€60, breakfast-€4, no fans, double-paned windows, just below train station and down the stairs at Via Fiume 143, tel. 0187-743-010, fax 0187-743-240, albergo parma@libero.it, some English spoken, Aurelio).

Private Rooms

Affitta camere, meaning rented rooms with no official reception, abound near the station. Expect good deals, modest English skills, and no breakfast (buy yourself a coffee and pastry at a nearby bar).

$$ La Stazione del Golfo dei Poeti rents four cute, clean, and contemporary rooms on the busy Via Fiume. Arrange to meet welcoming Rita outside the building or at the reception desk at Via Bixio 66—see map (Db-€80, cash only, air-con, Via Fiume 52, tel. 0187-714-416, mobile 345-352-6567, www.lastazionedelgolfodei poeti.it, info@lastazionedelgolfodeipoeti.it).

$$ Casa da Nè/Tre Frè, next door to the recommended Hotel Venezia, has 11 chic rooms with comfy linens and orange trees outside the door. It's located so close to the station that some rooms look out at the tracks; luckily, the windows are double-paned (Db-€80, air-con, Wi-Fi, Via Paleocapa 4, mobile 347-351-3239, www .trefre.it, info@trefre.it, Giovanna).

$$ L'Arca di Noè B&B is homey, with three bright and artsy rooms that share two bathrooms for one of the best deals on the Cinque Terre. A group could take the entire massive apartment (D-€50, Q-€80, includes breakfast, air-con, communal kitchen, 5-minute walk from station at Via Fiume 39, mobile 320-485-2434 or 348-916-9378, g.brunella@email.it, Brunella and Alessandra).

Near La Spezia

$$ Il Gelsomino, for drivers only, is a homey B&B in the hills above La Spezia overlooking the Gulf of Poets. It has three tranquil rooms: one with a bay-view terrace, one with hillside views, and a third that lacks views or a terrace. Don't confuse it with another

B&B called Il Gelsomino d'Oro (Db-€60, Tb-€90/Qb-€110, reconfirm a day in advance with your arrival time, large breakfast, Via dei Viseggi 9, tel. & fax 0187-704-201, www.ilgelsomino.biz, ilgelsomino@inwind.it, gracious Carla and Walter Massi).

$ **Santa Maria del Mare Monastery,** a last resort for drivers, rents 15 comfortable rooms to spiritual travelers high above La Spezia in a scenic but institutional setting (donation only, recommended offerings: dorm bed-€35, Db-€60, includes breakfast, additional €15/person for a meal, Via Montalbano 135B, tel. 0187-711-382, fax 0187-708-490, mobile 347-848-3993, www.santamaria delmare.it, madre@santamariadelmare.191.it).

Eating in La Spezia

Ristorante Roma da Marcellin, a one-minute walk from the station, has a cool, leafy terrace that's ideal for relaxing while you await your train. Grandpa Ottorino cooks up the freshest catch and a homemade filled pasta called *cappelletti* (daily 12:15-15:00 & 19:30-23:00; as you exit the station, turn left—it's across from Hotel Firenze e Continentale at Via Paleocapa 18; tel. 0187-715-921).

Il Pomodoro Pizzeria, just a few doors farther down on the corner of Via Zampino, offers more reasonable prices and an extensive selection of pizzas from €5. Practice your Italian with the chalkboard display of pastas of the day (Mon-Fri 12:00-14:00 & 19:00-23:00, Sat 19:00-23:00, closed Sun, Piazza S. Bon 5, tel. 0187-739-911).

La Spezia Connections

From La Spezia by Train to: Monterosso (2/hour, 25 minutes, €2.40), **Carrara** (2/hour, 25 minutes, €2.40), **Viareggio** (2/hour, 30-60 minutes, €4), **Pisa** (hourly, 1-1.5 hours, €5-9), **Florence** (4/day direct, otherwise nearly hourly, 2.5 hours, change in Pisa, €9), **Rome** (every 2 hours, 3.5-5 hours, €35-45), **Milan** (about hourly, 3 hours direct or with change in Genoa, €22-29), **Venice** (nearly hourly, 5 hours, 1-3 changes, €50-55).

By Bus to Portovenere: City buses generally depart from Viale Garibaldi (2/hour, 30 minutes, €1.90 each way, buy tickets at tobacco shops or newsstands, bus stop 11P—just past Corso Cavour; but note that Friday buses depart from Corso Cavour). From the La Spezia train station, exit left and head downhill, following the street to the first square (Piazza S. Bon). Continue down the pedestrian stretch of Via Fiume to Piazza Garibaldi, then turn right at the fountain in the square onto Viale Garibaldi; the bus stop for Portovenere-bound buses is after the first stoplight on the right side of the street. A timetable is posted by the bus stop.

Carrara

Perhaps the world's most famous marble quarries are just east of La Spezia in Carrara. Michelangelo himself traveled to these val-

leys to pick out the marble that he would work into his masterpieces. The towns of the region are dominated by marble. The quarries higher up are vast digs that dwarf the hardworking trucks and machinery coming and going. The **Marble Museum** traces the story of marble-cutting here from pre-

RIVIERA TOWNS

Roman times until today (€4.50, May-Sept Mon-Sat 9:30-13:00 & 15:30-18:00, Oct-April Mon-Sat 9:00-12:30 & 14:30-17:00, closed Sun year-round, Viale XX Settembre 85, tel. 0585-845-746, http://urano.isti.cnr.it:8880/museo/home.php).

For a guided visit, **Sara Paolini** is excellent (€80/half-day tour, mobile 373-711-6695, sarapaolini@hotmail.com). She is accustomed to meeting drivers at the Carrara freeway exit, or she can pick you up at the train station.

Portovenere

While the gritty port of La Spezia offers little in the way of redeeming touristic value, the nearby resort of Portovenere is enchanting. This Cinque Terre-esque village clings to a rocky promontory that juts into the sea and protects the harbor from the crashing waves. On the harbor, next to colorful bobbing boats, a row of restaurants—perfect for al fresco dining—feature local specialties such as *trenette* pasta with pesto and *spaghetti con frutti di mare*.

Local boats take you on a 40-minute excursion around three nearby islands or over to Lerici, the town across the bay. Lord Byron swam to Lerici (not recommended). Hardy hikers enjoy the five-hour (or more) hike to Riomaggiore, the nearest Cinque Terre town.

Getting There: Portovenere—not to be confused with Portofino—is an easy day trip from the Cinque Terre by **boat**

(Easter-Oct, 4-6/day 9:00-15:00, 1 hour, €12 one-way, €23 day pass includes hopping on and off and either Lerici or a jaunt around three small islands near Portovenere, www.navigazionegolfo deipoeti.it). You can also cruise between Portovenere and Santa Margherita Ligure, with stops in Vernazza and Sestri Levante, using another boat line (www.traghettiportofino.it. Pick up a schedule of departures and excursion options from the TI, or ask at your hotel. Or you can take the **bus** from La Spezia (2/hour, 30 minutes, €1.90, in La Spezia buy tickets at tobacco shops or newsstands; in Portovenere get tickets at TI). **Parking** is a nightmare here from May through September, but Albergo Il Genio offers free parking. In peak season, buses shuttle drivers from the parking lot just outside Portovenere to the harborside square. Otherwise, test your luck with the spots on the seaside (€1.50/hour).

Tourist Information: The TI is easy to find in the main square (June-Sept Thu-Tue 10:00-12:00 & 16:00-19:00, closed Wed; Oct-May Thu-Tue 10:00-12:00 & 15:00-18:00, closed Wed; Piazza Bastreri 7, tel. 0187-790-691).

Sleeping in Portovenere: If you've forgotten your yacht, try **$$$ Albergo Il Genio,** in the building where the main street hits the piazza (Db-€125, some rooms with views, no elevator, Internet access, free parking but request when you reserve, Piazza Bastreri 8, tel. & fax 0187-790-611, www.hotelgenioportovenere.com, info@hotelgenioportovenere.com). If your *vita* is feeling *dolce*, consider **$$$ Grand Hotel Portovenere,** which has striking sea views (from €121 for a viewless Db off-season to €280 for a view suite in summer, optional half-pension-€30-39/person, Internet access, tel. 0187-792-610, fax 0187-790-661, Via Garibaldi 5, www .portovenerehotel.it, ghp@village.it).

PRACTICALITIES

This section covers just the basics on traveling in Italy (for much more information, see *Rick Steves' Italy*). You can find free advice on specific topics at www.ricksteves.com/tips.

Money

Italy uses the euro currency: 1 euro (€) = about $1.40. To convert prices in euros to dollars, add about 40 percent: €20 = about $28, €50 = about $70. (Check www.oanda.com for the latest exchange rates.)

The standard way for travelers to get euros is to withdraw money from a cash machine (called a *bancomat* in Italy) using a debit or credit card, ideally with a Visa or MasterCard logo. Before departing, call your bank or credit-card company: Confirm that your card will work overseas, ask about international transaction fees, and alert them that you'll be making withdrawals in Europe.

Your US credit card might not work at some stores or at automated machines (e.g., train and subway ticket machines, luggage lockers, toll booths, parking garages, and self-serve gas pumps), because they're designed to accept European credit cards with a PIN code. If your card doesn't work, you have several options: Pay with euros, try your PIN code (ask your credit-card company in advance or use a debit card), or find a nearby cashier who should be able to process the transaction.

To keep your valuables safe, wear a money belt. But if you do lose your credit or debit card, report the loss immediately to the respective global customer-assistance centers. Call these 24-hour US numbers collect: Visa (410/581-9994), MasterCard (636/722-7111), and American Express (623/492-8427).

Phoning

Smart travelers use the telephone to reserve or reconfirm rooms, reserve restaurants, get directions, research transportation connections, confirm tour times, phone home, and lots more.

To call Italy from the US or Canada: Dial 011-39 and then the local number. (The 011 is our international access code, and 39 is Italy's country code.)

To call Italy from a European country: Dial 00-39 followed by the local number. (The 00 is Europe's international access code.)

To call within Italy: Just dial the local number.

To call from Italy to another country: Dial 00 followed by the country code (for example, 1 for the US or Canada), then the area code and number. If you're calling European countries whose phone numbers begin with 0, you'll usually have to omit that 0 when you dial.

Tips on Phoning: To make calls in Italy, you can buy two different types of phone cards—international or insertable—sold locally at newsstands. Cheap international phone cards, which work with a scratch-to-reveal PIN code at any phone, allow you to call home to the US for pennies a minute, and also work for domestic calls within Italy. Insertable phone cards, which must be inserted into public pay phones, are reasonable for calls within Italy (and work for international calls as well, but not as cheaply as the international phone cards). Calling from your hotel-room phone is usually expensive, unless you use an international phone card. A mobile phone—whether an American one that works in Italy, or a European one you buy when you arrive—is handy, but can be pricey. For more on phoning, see www.ricksteves.com/phoning.

Emergency Telephone Numbers in Italy: For English-speaking **police** help, dial 113. To summon an **ambulance,** call 118. For passport problems, call the **US Embassy** (in Rome, 24-hour line—tel. 06-46741) or **US Consulates** (Milan—tel. 02-290-351, Florence—tel. 055-266-951, Naples—tel. 081-583-8111); or the **Canadian Embassy** (in Rome, tel. 06-854-441) or **Canadian Consulates** (Naples—tel. 081-401-338, Padua—tel. 049-876-4833). For other concerns, get advice from your hotel.

Making Hotel Reservations

To ensure the best value, I recommend reserving rooms in advance, particularly during peak season. Email the hotelier with the following key pieces of information: number and type of rooms; number of nights; date of arrival; date of departure; and any special requests. (For a sample form, see www.ricksteves.com/reservation.) Use the European style for writing dates: day/month/year. For example, for a two-night stay in July, you could request: "1 double room for 2 nights, arrive 16/07/12, depart 18/07/12." Hoteliers typically ask for your credit-card number as a deposit.

In general, hotel prices can soften if you do any of the following: offer to pay cash, stay at least three nights, mention this book, or travel off-season. You can also try asking for a cheaper room (for example, with a bathroom down the hall), or offer to skip breakfast.

Eating

Italy offers a wide array of eateries. A *ristorante* is a formal restaurant, while a *trattoria* or *osteria* is usually more traditional and simpler (but can still be pricey). Italian "bars" are not taverns, but small cafés selling sandwiches, coffee, and other drinks. An *enoteca* is a wine bar with snacks and light meals. Take-away food from pizza shops and delis (such as a *rosticceria* or *tavola calda*) makes an easy picnic.

Italians eat dinner a bit later than we do; better restaurants start serving around 19:00. A full meal consists of an appetizer (antipasto), a first course (*primo piatto*, pasta or soup), and a second course (*secondo piatto*, expensive meat and fish dishes). Vegetables *(verdure)* may come with the *secondo* or cost extra, as a side dish (*contorni*). The euros can add up in a hurry, but you don't have to order each course. My approach is to mix antipasti and *primi piatti* family-style with my dinner partners (skipping *secondi*). Or, for unexciting but basic values, look for a *menù turistico* (or *menù del giorno*), a three- or four-course, fixed-price meal deal.

Good service is relaxed (slow to an American). You won't get the bill until you ask for it: *"Il conto?"* Most restaurants include a service charge in their prices (check the menu for *servizio incluso*—generally around 15 percent). If the menu states *servizio non incluso*, or *servizio* with a specific percentage, a fixed percentage (usually 10–15 percent of the total) will be added as a line item to the bottom of the bill. In either case, the total you pay already includes a basic tip. To reward good service, you can round up to the nearest euro.

At bars and cafés, getting a drink while standing at the bar (*banco)* is cheaper than drinking it at a table *(tavolo)* or sitting outside *(terrazza)*. This tiered pricing system is clearly posted on the wall. Sometimes you'll pay at a cash register, then take the receipt to another counter to claim your drink.

Transportation

By Train: In Italy, most travelers find it's cheapest simply to buy train tickets as they go. To see if a railpass could save you money, check www.ricksteves.com/rail. To research train schedules, visit Germany's excellent all-Europe website, http://bahn.hafas.de/bin /query.exe/en, or Italy's www.trenitalia.com (domestic journeys only).

You can buy tickets at train stations (at the ticket window or at automated machines with English instructions) or from travel agencies. Before boarding the train, you must validate your train documents by stamping them in the yellow box near the platform. Strikes *(sciopero)* are common and generally announced in advance (but a few sporadic trains still run—ask around).

By Car: It's cheaper to arrange most car rentals from the US. For tips on your insurance options, see www.ricksteves.com /cdw. Theft insurance is mandatory in Italy ($15–20/day). Bring your driver's license. You're also technically required to have an International Driving Permit—a translation of your driver's license (sold at your local AAA office for $15 plus the cost of two passport-type photos; see www.aaa.com). For route planning, try www.viamichelin.com. Italy's freeway *(autostrada)* system is slick and speedy, but you'll pay about a dollar for every 10 minutes of use. Be warned that car traffic is restricted in many city centers—don't drive or park in any area that has a sign reading *Zona Traffico Limitato* (*ZTL*, often shown above a red circle)...or you might be mailed a ticket later. A car is a worthless headache in cities—park it safely (get tips from your hotel). As break-ins are common, be sure all of your valuables are out of sight and locked in the trunk, or even better, with you or in your hotel room.

Helpful Hints

Theft Alert: Italy has particularly hardworking pickpockets. Assume beggars are pickpockets and any scuffle is simply a distraction by a team of thieves. If you stop for any commotion or show, put your hands in your pockets before someone else does. Better yet, wear a money belt.

Time: Italy uses the 24-hour clock. It's the same through 12:00 noon, then keep going: 13:00, 14:00, and so on. Italy, like most of continental Europe, is six/nine hours ahead of the East/ West Coasts of the US.

Business Hours: Many businesses are open throughout the day Monday through Saturday, but some businesses close for lunch (roughly 13:00-15:30), particularly in smaller towns.

Sights: Opening and closing hours of sights can change unexpectedly; confirm the latest times with the local tourist information office or its website. Some major churches enforce a modest dress code (no bare shoulders or shorts) for everyone, even children.

Holidays and Festivals: Italy celebrates many holidays, which can close sights and attract crowds (book hotel rooms ahead). For information on holidays and festivals, check Italy's website: www.italiantourism.com. For a simple list showing major—though not all—events, see www.ricksteves.com/festivals.

Numbers and Stumblers: What Americans call the second floor of a building is the first floor in Europe. Europeans write dates as day/month/year, so Christmas is 25/12/12. Commas are decimal points and vice versa—a dollar and a half is 1,50, a thousand is 1.000, and there are 5.280 feet in a mile. Italy uses the metric system: A kilogram is 2.2 pounds; a liter is about a quart; and a kilometer is six-tenths of a mile.

PRACTICALITIES

Resources from Rick Steves

This Snapshot guide is excerpted from the latest edition of *Rick Steves' Italy*, which is one of more than 30 titles in my series of guidebooks on European travel. I also produce a public television series, *Rick Steves' Europe*, and a public radio show, *Travel with Rick Steves*. My website, www.ricksteves.com, offers free travel information, a Graffiti Wall for travelers' comments, guidebook updates, my travel blog, an online travel store, and information on European railpasses and our tours of Europe. If you're bringing a mobile device on your trip, you can download free information from Rick Steves Audio Europe, featuring podcasts of my radio shows, free audio tours of major sights in Europe, and travel interviews and other audio content about Italy (via www.ricksteves.com/audioeurope, iTunes, or the Rick Steves Audio Europe free smartphone app).

Additional Resources
Tourist Information: www.italiantourism.com
Passports and Red Tape: www.travel.state.gov
Packing List: www.ricksteves.com/packlist
Cheap Flights: www.skyscanner.net
Airplane Carry-on Restrictions: www.tsa.gov/travelers
Updates for This Book: www.ricksteves.com/update

How Was Your Trip?

If you'd like to share your tips, concerns, and discoveries after using this book, please fill out the survey at www.ricksteves.com/feedback. Thanks in advance—it helps a lot.

Italian Survival Phrases

Good day.	**Buon giorno.**	bwohn JOR-noh
Do you speak English?	**Parla inglese?**	PAR-lah een-GLAY-zay
Yes. / No.	**Si. / No.**	see / noh
I (don't) understand.	**(Non) capisco.**	(nohn) kah-PEES-koh
Please.	**Per favore.**	pehr fah-VOH-ray
Thank you.	**Grazie.**	GRAHT-seeay
You're welcome.	**Prego.**	PRAY-go
I'm sorry.	**Mi dispiace.**	mee dee-speeAH-chay
Excuse me.	**Mi scusi.**	mee SKOO-zee
(No) problem.	**(Non) c'è un problema.**	(nohn) cheh oon proh-BLAY-mah
Good.	**Va bene.**	vah BEHN-ay
Goodbye.	**Arrivederci.**	ah-ree-vay-DEHR-chee
one / two	**uno / due**	OO-noh / DOO-ay
three / four	**tre / quattro**	tray / KWAH-troh
five / six	**cinque / sei**	CHEENG-kway / SEHee
seven / eight	**sette / otto**	SEHT-tay / OT-toh
nine / ten	**nove / dieci**	NOV-ay / deeAY-chee
How much is it?	**Quanto costa?**	KWAHN-toh KOS-tah
Write it?	**Me lo scrive?**	may loh SKREE-vay
Is it free?	**È gratis?**	eh GRAH-tees
Is it included?	**È incluso?**	eh een-KLOO-zoh
Where can I buy / find...?	**Dove posso comprare / trovare...?**	DOH-vay POS-soh kohm-PRAH-ray / troh-VAH-ray
I'd like / We'd like...	**Vorrei / Vorremmo...**	vor-REHee / vor-RAY-moh
...a room.	**...una camera.**	OO-nah KAH-meh-rah
...a ticket to ___.	**...un biglietto per ___.**	oon beel-YEHT-toh pehr
Is it possible?	**È possibile?**	eh poh-SEE-bee-lay
Where is...?	**Dov'è...?**	DOH-veh
...the train station	**...la stazione**	lah staht-seeOH-nay
...the bus station	**...la stazione degli autobus**	lah staht-seeOH-nay DAYL-yee OW-toh-boos
...tourist information	**...informazioni per turisti**	een-for-maht-seeOH-nee pehr too-REE-stee
...the toilet	**...la toilette**	lah twah-LEHT-tay
men	**uomini, signori**	WOH-mee-nee, seen-YOH-ree
women	**donne, signore**	DON-nay, seen-YOH-ray
left / right	**sinistra / destra**	see-NEE-strah / DEHS-trah
straight	**sempre diritto**	SEHM-pray dee-REE-toh
When do you open / close?	**A che ora aprite / chiudete?**	ah kay OH-rah ah-PREE-tay / keeoo-DAY-tay
At what time?	**A che ora?**	ah kay OH-rah
Just a moment.	**Un momento.**	oon moh-MAYN-toh
now / soon / later	**adesso / presto / tardi**	ah-DEHS-soh / PREHS-toh / TAR-dee
today / tomorrow	**oggi / domani**	OH-jee / doh-MAH-nee

PRACTICALITIES

In an Italian Restaurant

I'd like...	Vorrei...	vor-REHee
We'd like...	Vorremmo...	vor-RAY-moh
...to reserve...	...prenotare...	pray-noh-TAH-ray
...a table for one / two.	...un tavolo per uno / due.	oon TAH-voh-loh pehr OO-noh / DOO-ay
Non-smoking.	Non fumare.	nohn foo-MAH-ray
Is this seat free?	È libero questo posto?	eh LEE-bay-roh KWEHS-toh POH-stoh
The menu (in English), please.	Il menù (in inglese), per favore.	eel may-NOO (een een-GLAY-zay) pehr fah-VOH-ray
service (not) included	servizio (non) incluso	sehr-VEET-seeoh (nohn) een-KLOO-zoh
cover charge	pane e coperto	PAH-nay ay koh-PEHR-toh
to go	da portar via	dah POR-tar VEE-ah
with / without	con / senza	kohn / SEHN-sah
and / or	e / o	ay / oh
menu (of the day)	menù (del giorno)	may-NOO (dayl JOR-noh)
specialty of the house	specialità della casa	spay-chah-lee-TAH DEHL-lah KAH-zah
first course (pasta, soup)	primo piatto	PREE-moh peeAH-toh
main course (meat, fish)	secondo piatto	say-KOHN-doh peeAH-toh
side dishes	contorni	kohn-TOR-nee
bread	pane	PAH-nay
cheese	formaggio	for-MAH-joh
sandwich	panino	pah-NEE-noh
soup	minestra, zuppa	mee-NEHS-trah, TSOO-pah
salad	insalata	een-sah-LAH-tah
meat	carne	KAR-nay
chicken	pollo	POH-loh
fish	pesce	PEH-shay
seafood	frutti di mare	FROO-tee dee MAH-ray
fruit / vegetables	frutta / legumi	FROO-tah / lay-GOO-mee
dessert	dolci	DOHL-chee
tap water	acqua del rubinetto	AH-kwah dayl roo-bee-NAY-toh
mineral water	acqua minerale	AH-kwah mee-nay-RAH-lay
milk	latte	LAH-tay
(orange) juice	succo (d'arancia)	SOO-koh (dah-RAHN-chah)
coffee / tea	caffè / tè	kah-FEH / teh
wine	vino	VEE-noh
red / white	rosso / bianco	ROH-soh / beeAHN-koh
glass / bottle	bicchiere / bottiglia	bee-keeAY-ray / boh-TEEL-yah
beer	birra	BEE-rah
Cheers!	Cin cin!	cheen cheen
More. / Another.	Ancora un po.' / Un altro.	ahn-KOH-rah oon poh / oon AHL-troh
The same.	Lo stesso.	loh STEHS-soh
The bill, please.	Il conto, per favore.	eel KOHN-toh pehr fah-VOH-ray
tip	mancia	MAHN-chah
Delicious!	Delizioso!	day-leet-seeOH-zoh

For more user-friendly Italian phrases, check out *Rick Steves' Italian Phrase Book & Dictionary* or *Rick Steves' French, Italian, and German Phrase Book*.

INDEX

INDEX

Audio Europe

RICK STEVES AUDIO EUROPE

Rick's free app and podcasts

The FREE **Rick Steves Audio Europe**™ app for iPhone, iPad and iPod Touch gives you 29 self-guided audio tours of Europe's top museums, sights and historic walks—plus more than 200 tracks filled with cultural insights and sightseeing tips from Rick's radio interviews—all organized into geographic-specific playlists.

Let **Rick Steves Audio Europe**™ amplify your guidebook.

With Rick whispering in your ear Europe gets even better.

Thanks Facebook fans for submitting photos while on location! From top: John Kuijper in Florence, Brenda Mamer with her mother in Rome, Angel Capobianco in London, and Alyssa Passey with her friend in Paris.

Find out more at ricksteves.com

Join a Rick Steves tour

Enjoy Europe's warmest welcome... with the flexibility and friendship of a small group getting to know Rick's favorite places and people. It all starts with our free tour catalog and DVD.

Great guides, small groups, no grumps.

▶ Plan Your Trip

Browse thousands of articles and a wealth of money-saving tips for planning your dream trip. You'll find up-to-date information on Europe's best destinations, packing smart, getting around, finding rooms, staying healthy, avoiding scams and more.

▶ Eurail Passes

Find out, step-by-step, if a railpass makes sense for your trip—and how to avoid buying more than you need. Get free shipping on online orders

▶ Graffiti Wall & Travelers Helpline

Learn, ask, share—our online community of savvy travelers is a great resource for first-time travelers to Europe, as well as seasoned pros.

Rick Steves.

www.ricksteves.com

EUROPE GUIDES

Best of Europe
Eastern Europe
Europe Through the Back Door
Mediterranean Cruise Ports

COUNTRY GUIDES

Croatia & Slovenia
England
France
Germany
Great Britain
Ireland
Italy
Portugal
Scandinavia
Spain
Switzerland

CITY & REGIONAL GUIDES

Amsterdam, Bruges & Brussels
Budapest
Florence & Tuscany
Greece: Athens & the Peloponnese
Istanbul
London
Paris
Prague & the Czech Republic
Provence & the French Riviera
Rome
Venice
Vienna, Salzburg & Tirol

SNAPSHOT GUIDES

Barcelona
Berlin
Bruges & Brussels
Copenhagen & the Best of
    Denmark
Dublin
Dubrovnik
Hill Towns of Central Italy
Italy's Cinque Terre
Krakow, Warsaw & Gdansk
Lisbon
Madrid & Toledo
Munich, Bavaria & Salzburg
Naples & the Amalfi Coast
Northern Ireland
Norway
Scotland
Sevilla, Granada & Southern Spain
Stockholm

POCKET GUIDES

London
Paris
Rome

TRAVEL CULTURE

Europe 101
European Christmas
Postcards from Europe
Travel as a Political Act

Rick Steves guidebooks are published by Avalon Travel,
a member of the Perseus Books Group.

NOW AVAILABLE:
eBOOKS, APPS & BLU-RAY

eBOOKS

Most guides are available as eBooks from Amazon, Barnes & Noble, Borders, Apple, and Sony. Free apps for eBook reading are available in the Apple App Store and Android Market, and eBook readers such as Kindle, Nook, and Kobo all have free apps that work on smartphones.

RICK STEVES' EUROPE DVDs

10 New Shows 2011–2012
Austria & the Alps
Eastern Europe
England & Wales
European Christmas
European Travel Skills & Specials
France
Germany, BeNeLux & More
Greece & Turkey
Iran
Ireland & Scotland
Italy's Cities
Italy's Countryside
Scandinavia
Spain
Travel Extras

BLU-RAY

Celtic Charms
Eastern Europe Favorites
European Christmas
Italy Through the Back Door
Mediterranean Mosaic
Surprising Cities of Europe

PHRASE BOOKS & DICTIONARIES

French
French, Italian & German
German
Italian
Portuguese
Spanish

JOURNALS

Rick Steves' Pocket Travel Journal
Rick Steves' Travel Journal

APPS

Select Rick Steves guides are available as apps in the Apple App Store.

PLANNING MAPS

Britain, Ireland & London
Europe
France & Paris
Germany, Austria & Switzerland
Ireland
Italy
Spain & Portugal

Avalon Travel
a member of the Perseus Books Group
1700 Fourth Street
Berkeley, CA 94710

Printed in the United States by Worzalla.

ISBN 978-1-59880-684-7

For the latest on Rick's lectures, guidebooks, tours, public radio show, and public television
series, contact Europe Through the Back Door, Box 2009, Edmonds, WA 98020, tel.
425/771-8303, fax 425/771-0833, www.ricksteves.com, rick@ricksteves.com.

Europe Through the Back Door Reviewing Editors: Risa Laib, Jennifer Madison Davis,
    Cameron Hewitt
ETBD Editors: Gretchen Strauch, Cathy McDonald, Suzanne Kotz, Cathy Lu, Tom
    Griffin
Research Assistance: Ian Watson, Ben Cameron, Karin Kibby, Helen Inman, Kat Reno,
    Claire Burns
Avalon Travel Senior Editor and Series Manager: Madhu Prasher
Avalon Travel Project Editor: Kelly Lydick
Copy Editor: Patrick Collins
Proofreader: Nöel Chrisman
Indexer: Stephen Callahan
Production and Typesetting: McGuire Barber Design
Cover Design: Kimberly Glyder Design
Graphic Content Director: Laura VanDeventer
Maps & Graphics: David C. Hoerlein, Laura VanDeventer, Twozdai Hulse, Lauren Mills,
    Barb Geisler, Kat Bennett, Mike Morgenfeld, Brice Ticen
Photography: Rick Steves, Gene Openshaw, David C. Hoerlein, Laura VanDeventer,
    Cameron Hewitt, Jennifer Hauseman, Dominic Bonuccelli, Michael Potter, Les
    Wahlstrom, Robyn Cronin, Ben Cameron, Ian Watson, Bruce VanDeventer, Anne
    Jenkins, Wikimedia Commons
Cover Photo: Riomaggiore at Dusk in Cinque Terre, Italy © Bill Grove/istockphoto.com
Title Page Photo: aerial view of Vernazza, Cinque Terre, Italy © Tim Wege/www.123rf.com
Page 1 Photo: Italy's Cinque Terre coastline © Oxana Morozova/www.123rf.com

ABOUT THE AUTHOR

RICK STEVES

 Since 1973, Rick Steves has spent 100 days every year exploring Europe. Rick produces a public television series (*Rick Steves' Europe*), a public radio show (*Travel with Rick Steves*), and an app and podcast (*Rick Steves Audio Europe*); writes a bestselling series of guidebooks and a nationally syndicated newspaper column; organizes guided tours that take over ten thousand travelers to Europe annually; and offers an information-packed website (www.ricksteves.com). With the help of his hardworking staff of 80 at Europe Through the Back Door—in Edmonds, Washington, just north of Seattle—Rick's mission is to make European travel fun, affordable, and culturally enlightening for Americans.

Want More Italy?
Maximize the experience with Rick Steves as your guide

Guidebooks
Rome, Florence, Venice and Italy guides make side-trips smooth and affordable

Phrase Books
Rely on Rick's Italian Phrase Book and Dictionary

Rick's DVDs
Preview where you're going with 13 shows on Italy

Rick's Audio Europe™ App
Get free audio tours for Italy's top sights

Small-Group Tours
Rick offers several great itineraries through Italy

For all the details, visit ricksteves.com